LESSON DESIGN

for

Differentiated Instruction,

Grades 4–9

LESSON DESIGN

for

Differentiated Instruction,

Grades 4–9

KATHY TUCHMAN GLASS

Foreword by H. Lynn Erickson

CORWIN
A SAGE Company

For information:

Corwin
A SAGE Company
2455 Teller Road
Thousand Oaks, California 91320
(800) 233-9936
Fax: (800) 417-2466
www.corwinpress.com

SAGE India Pvt. Ltd.
B 1/I 1 Mohan Cooperative
 Industrial Area
Mathura Road, New Delhi 110 044
India

SAGE Ltd.
1 Oliver's Yard
55 City Road
London EC1Y 1SP
United Kingdom

SAGE Asia-Pacific Pte. Ltd.
33 Pekin Street #02-01
Far East Square
Singapore 048763

Printed in the United States of America

Library of Congress Cataloging-in-Publication Data

Glass, Kathy Tuchman.
Lesson design for differentiated instruction, grades 4-9 / Kathy Tuchman Glass; foreword by H. Lynn Erickson.
   p. cm.
Includes bibliographical references and index.
ISBN 978-1-4129-5981-0 (cloth)
ISBN 978-1-4129-5982-7 (pbk.)
   1. Lesson planning. 2. Individualized instruction. I. Title.

LB1027.4.G53 2009
372.13028—dc22   2008036424

This book is printed on acid-free paper.

09 10 11 12 13 10 9 8 7 6 5 4 3 2 1

Acquisitions Editor:	Cathy Hernandez
Editorial Assistant:	Sarah Bartlett
Production Editor:	Jane Haenel
Copy Editor:	Cheryl Rivard
Typesetter:	C&M Digitals (P) Ltd.
Proofreader:	Theresa Kay
Indexer:	Molly Hall
Cover and Graphic Designer:	Scott Van Atta

Contents

List of Figures

Foreword

Kathy Glass is a teachers' teacher. And her book, *Lesson Design for Differentiated Instruction, Grades 4–9*, is an invaluable teacher tool. How many of us as educators remember slogging through our preservice "methods classes" to learn how to design and teach instructional units and lessons? It was more often a sterile exercise since we had not yet experienced the exciting dynamics of the classroom. We tried to design activities to meet curricular "objectives," but with little or no actual classroom experience we felt like creative writers suffering from insecurity complexes. How I wish Kathy Glass and her book had been available to help me learn how to design quality differentiated, instructional lessons!

Lesson Design for Differentiated Instruction, Grades 4–9, is a current and timely book reflecting the latest research and thinking on quality designs for learning. Kathy presents in a clear and accessible way the thinking and ideas of noted national researchers and educators, like Carol Ann Tomlinson on differentiated curriculum and instruction. But she extends their work and makes her own mark by combining different ideas to create a solid lesson planner that incorporates standards, guiding questions, concepts, skills and activities, resources/materials, timing, grouping suggestions, teaching strategies, differentiation suggestions, extensions, and assessments. Kathy provides a war chest of valuable concrete examples to illustrate the components that make up her lesson design. She encourages teachers to adapt and apply the many examples to fit their own curricula and classrooms. Kathy also includes numerous completed lesson plans for different subject areas. She is an educational generalist who is able to work across subjects. Her powerful examples for a variety of subject areas give this book broad appeal.

Lesson Design for Differentiated Instruction, Grades 4–9, is packed with ideas, examples, and tools to teach and aid an instructor. The writing style is exceptionally clear and focused. Sentences are concise and to the point. The flow of the ideas, the logical organization of the text, and the illustrative examples throughout allow the reader to relate to, and enjoy, the reading experience. It is easy to visualize the lessons as they would play out in the classroom, and the teacher can easily see how to adapt activities or questions to his or her own instruction.

One thing that made this book so outstanding was the amazing number of support materials from the lesson-planning template to ways to differentiate, to student response guides across subject areas, to multiple kinds of assessments A–Z, and rubrics. This is a teacher's candy store. I have been an educator for more than four decades and I was still excited to examine the tremendous wealth of support materials found in this book.

Lesson Design for Differentiated Instruction, Grades 4–9, is a solid performance of the author's knowledge and understanding in the area of curriculum design, instruction, and current research. For example, many educators think that a statement like "Analyze the history of Native Americans" is a skill. But Kathy Glass understands that skills need to transfer across many examples; that when we tie a skill to a topic, we have stated the content objective or the activity. The skill would be "Analyze primary and secondary source documents." This skill can be applied to understand the history of Native Americans as well as to develop the skill. Of course, teachers need to *develop* the skill within the context of particular content; but they also need to internalize the "skill set" for the subject or subjects they teach so that they can transfer the different skills across many applications in their designs for learning. Learning how to articulate rich, discipline-specific skills that can be applied across different applications is a skill in itself.

Another indicator of this author's expertise is her clear statement that differentiation does not mean "dumbing down" curriculum and instruction for struggling students. She tells teachers that the expectation of differentiated instruction is that all students have equally engaging work; and though tasks may be diverse to meet different readiness levels, learning styles, and interests, the goals are the same for all students.

This book further emphasizes the importance and power of guiding questions. Kathy provides many subject-specific examples for unit-level and lesson-level guiding questions. She teaches us how to design quality questions and guides us in learning how to use questions to focus learning, deepen understanding, and tie them in to required standards.

Teachers are always looking for that great lesson plan. They scour the Internet and commercial materials and gather what they can find that relates to the topics they teach. But they are often disappointed when they try out the lesson. There is something missing. Kathy understands that the best lessons are designed by the teacher who is going to do the instructing. They know their students best—their learning preferences, their readiness profiles, and their interests. Kathy's book gives a teacher everything he or she needs to design excellent lessons that are differentiated and conceptually focused. She is the support for teachers who want to be architects for learning—who want to combine the science and art of teaching as the design for instruction. Yes, I wish Kathy had been my "teacher of teachers."

H. Lynn Erickson
Educational Consultant and Author

Preface

Formerly a middle school teacher, I now consult with K–12 teachers in areas of curriculum and instruction, such as curriculum mapping, differentiation, curriculum design, instructional strategies, and so forth. In my experience, I have encountered teachers who labor arduously to perfect their craft and want support to further their professional learning. Additionally, I have mentored teachers who are anxious to work hard but have not been exposed to the proper resources and materials to know where to put their energy in creating meaningful, differentiated curriculum. Often I coach or present to teachers who are forever seeking ways to engage students and make learning fruitful. It could be that the teacher is unaware of how to differentiate, so she teaches to the middle and fails to entice those at the other ends of the learning spectrum. Or it could be (a) that the teacher conducts lessons and activities in isolation so the students cannot make connections for the greater purpose of their work, (b) that she does not have at her disposal a variety of instructional strategies to make learning varied and engaging, or (c) that she has an arsenal of instructional strategies but wants an infusion of new ways to present material. For whatever reason teachers come to me, the overriding common denominator is that they are on a constant search to improve and refine what they do so all students are challenged and enlightened.

I am also a mother of two children—a daughter in middle school and a son in high school. They couldn't be any more diverse in their approaches to homework and school. My daughter dashes to complete her homework the minute she gets home from any extracurricular activity. Her social time with friends after school revolves around homework as she and her friends all conscientiously complete their assigned tasks amidst handfuls of popcorn and some giggling mixed with chatter. My son, on the other hand, takes an eternity to finish his homework and finds any excuse to delay the dreaded undertaking. He will prolong a mediocre dessert pretending it is a luscious treat, or he will insist that a shower is imperative and extend the typical time it takes to wash just to postpone homework. "Stop dawdling and get to work," my husband repeatedly tells him with irritation punctuating each word. The differences among my kids are not unlike the differences we all experience in the classroom. It is a reality at home and in the classroom. The experience I share with you is as a former teacher, a consultant, and a mother who is acutely aware of the challenges in the classroom to make learning innovative, meaningful, and differentiated.

This book is intended to help teachers write and deliver more meaningful lessons in fourth- to ninth-grade classrooms and differentiate the curriculum to appeal to all levels, interests, and characteristics of learners. Students should leave a classroom energized about what they learn, understand the implications of the unit at hand, and make connections. If it is a worksheet that a teacher assigns, then that worksheet needs to have some valuable meaning and connect to something greater. If vocabulary or concept words are part of an assignment, then those words should be used repeatedly in many contexts to make students own and use them naturally in speaking and writing. If it is a particular skill a teacher wishes to impart, then students should see how it connects to what they are learning in this or other classes or the world at large so it isn't a skill taught in isolation. Each and every assignment and activity should have a greater meaning, and students should leave a classroom knowing the answer to that meaning and its application at whatever level they are able.

Classrooms are filled with opportunities for rich curriculum. It is my hope that through this book, teachers will develop a stronger sense of how to craft differentiated lessons so they can impart knowledge in a more thoughtful, effective manner to help all students find value and meaning in that curriculum. Conducting lessons that stimulate thought and intrigue students can help put an end to blank stares and noncommittal shrugs. Although, being a former teacher myself and a mother of school-age children, it is often hard to ignite passion where there is much competition at stake for teachers. Unfortunately, educators have to work harder to craft and deliver enticing, meaningful curriculum because many students at this age have a multitude of preoccupations in their lives.

The work presented here is culled from my sense of how to differentiate from reading and studying the works of various experts in this field and from my teacher clients. I have learned a great deal from Carol Tomlinson and also from Carolyn Chapman, Susan Winebrenner, Lynn Erickson, Pattie Drapeau, and others. Since I interface with teachers most days, I am fortunate that my work goes into immediate action in the classroom. I help teachers differentiate their lessons and revise after they have learned what happens in the trenches. This process of working with them and hearing their feedback also fuels me with knowledge. This book takes you through what I have learned to do after researching, teaching, talking with teachers, and observing student work and students. I have my own method for how to differentiate lessons that I present to you here along with what I've gleaned from others. What I have written is based on sound research from the experts in differentiation and curriculum I've created that teachers have implemented. I think all teachers have levels of expertise. What I propose is to bring each teacher's level of expertise up several rungs.

Inside these pages, you will find components of curriculum design and numerous lessons for upper-elementary to ninth-grade curriculum that (1) incorporate the tenets of sound lesson planning, (2) include differentiation, (3) follow a lesson template, and (4) can be adapted to fit the goals of your particular curriculum. As you read this book, my hope is that you grow professionally and become more astute as you do the following and even more:

- Teach lessons in this book and critique what worked and did not work, then adapt accordingly.

- Critically look at curriculum you have crafted to ask yourself how it can be more meaningful for all students.

- Ask yourself how you can specifically differentiate particular lessons you teach to better meet students' needs.

- Review lessons you teach and identify the concrete reasons for teaching them. In other words, articulate the overarching standards and essential questions that guide your curriculum, identify and create various assessments that allow students to demonstrate what they have learned and provide information for differentiating, and conduct differentiated activities and lessons that link to the lesson and unit goals.

Below is a brief overview of what each chapter entails:

- *Chapter 1: Differentiated Instruction and Strategies*—Differentiation is clearly defined as well as the rationale for using it. Various strategies for the types of differentiation are presented along with cursory ideas on how to use each one. This is a foundational chapter for the entire book and can be used as a reference after reading.

- *Chapter 2: Differentiated Lesson Design*—This chapter features a lesson template and comprehensive, differentiated lesson examples for core content areas. Peruse all examples even if you do not teach a particular content area of a lesson shown. It will give you exposure to differentiation in action that you can possibly apply.

- *Chapter 3: Standards, Concepts, and Guiding Questions*—In this chapter, I define guiding questions, illustrate how to use standards and concepts to create these questions, and provide a number of examples. In short, the focus for this chapter is intertwining the trio of questions, standards, and concepts as the basis for creating sound curriculum.

- *Chapter 4: Assessment in a Differentiated Classroom*—The focus for this chapter is on several assessments that can be used in lesson and unit design. I provide many concrete examples in addition to ideas for how to use, adapt, and differentiate the featured assessments.

- *Chapter 5: Additional Lesson-Planning Components for Differentiated Curriculum*—The remaining lesson components from the initially presented lesson template of Chapter 2 are featured here. I explain each component, provide examples, and suggest ways to differentiate.

- *Chapter 6: Closing*—This brief chapter brings closure to the book and a call to action for teachers interested in differentiating instruction.

Acknowledgments

I have worked with many dedicated teachers who understand the need for differentiation. They have eagerly put the work I present to them into action and collaborate with me to produce effective and meaningful differentiated curriculum. I gratefully acknowledge these teachers who know who they are and teach in these locations:

- Menlo Park Elementary School District (Menlo Park, CA)
- Corte Madera School (Portola Valley, CA)
- Bernardo Heights Middle School (San Diego, CA)
- Burlingame Intermediate School (Burlingame, CA)
- Santa Clara Unified School District (Santa Clara, CA)
- La Entrada School (Menlo Park, CA)

My husband, Mike, is unfailingly supportive of the work I do, which helps to spur me on to greater heights.

I thank the reviewers who took the time and energy to scrupulously review my manuscript and carefully comment on my work. I particularly thank my editor, Cathy Hernandez, who championed me along and provided keen insights.

Lyneille Meza
Algebra 1 Teacher
Guyer High School
Denton, TX

Judith J. Onslow
Science Specialist, Curriculum and Instruction
Anchorage School District
Anchorage, AK

Terry Tomasek
Assistant Professor
Department of Teacher Education
Elon University
Elon, NC

Jude Huntz
Adult Education/RCIA Coordinator
St. Michael the Archangel Catholic Parish
Leawood, KS

Thank you Modell Marlow Andersen and Allan Varni for taking the time to read my book and shed light on the essential elements.

I am infinitely grateful to Lynn Erickson for her careful reading of my manuscript and the merit she found in my work. Her endorsement of what I wrote means a great deal to me.

About the Author

As a former master teacher who holds current teaching certification, **Kathy Tuchman Glass** consults with schools and districts, presents at conferences, and teaches seminars for university and county programs delivering customized professional development. Kathy has been in education for 20 years and works with teachers at all levels and in groups of varying sizes from one-on-one to entire school districts. She assists administrators and teachers with strategic planning to determine school or district objectives, and presents and collaborates on designing standards-based differentiated curriculum, crafting essential understandings and guiding questions, using compelling instructional strategies that engage all learners, incorporating various effective assessments into curriculum, using six-trait writing instruction and assessment, creating curriculum maps, and more.

In addition to *Lesson Design for Differentiated Instruction, Grades 4–9,* Kathy has written *Curriculum Mapping: A Step-by-Step Guide to Creating Curriculum Year Overviews* (2007) and *Curriculum Design for Writing Instruction: Creating Standards-Based Lesson Plans and Rubrics* (2005). She is currently coauthoring with Cindy Strickland a professional development guide on *The Parallel Curriculum Model.* In addition, Kathy has served as a reader and reviewer for *Reader's Handbook: A Student Guide for Reading and Learning* (2002) and as a contributing writer and consultant for the Heath Middle Level Literature series (1995).

Originally from Indianapolis, Kathy resides in the San Francisco Bay Area with her supportive husband and two loving and energetic teenagers. She can be reached by phone at 650-366-8122 or through her e-mail at kathy@kathyglassconsulting.com. Her Web site is www.kathy glassconsulting.com.

This book is dedicated to Carol Tomlinson. Your expertise, humility, and generosity of time and spirit have had an immeasurable impact on my work.

1

Differentiated Instruction and Strategies

This book focuses on creating differentiated lessons and not entire units of study. It is imperative that teachers understand not only the overarching goals of a given lesson but also the broader unit of study before diving in and teaching. The backward design model emphasizes beginning with the end in mind. In their book *Integrating Differentiated Instruction + Understanding by Design,* authors Carol Tomlinson and Jay McTighe (2006) write: "The concept of planning backward from desired results is not new. In 1949, Ralph Tyler described this approach as an effective process for focusing instruction. More recently, Stephen Covey (1989) in the best-selling book *Seven Habits of Highly Effective People,* reports that effective people in various fields are goal oriented and plan with the end in mind. Although not a new idea, we have found that the deliberate use of backward design for planning courses, units, and individual lessons results in more clearly defined goals, more appropriate assessments, and more purposeful teaching." Typically, we think of applying backward design to comprehensive units of study. But since the notion of this design process is essentially a sequence for curriculum, employing backward design to each lesson is prudent so teachers know what direction a lesson is headed by looking at the final goal first. One way to do this is by creating guiding questions that emanate from standards to use as a guidepost in devising lessons. Using these questions allows teachers to be more effective in teaching by focusing a lesson on standards and concepts so students can grasp the overarching goals.

In this book, teachers will find a multitude of differentiated lessons tied to a curriculum for fourth- to ninth-grade students. Each lesson includes the tenets of backward design in that they begin with clearly articulated standards and guiding questions. Subsequently, I include details to execute lessons including student groupings, strategies, assessments, resources, student handouts, suggestions for differentiation, and more.

DIFFERENTIATED INSTRUCTION

The term *differentiation* and its use in the classroom are familiar to many educators. There are innumerable books, articles, Web sites, and other resources dedicated to differentiation. Extensive lists of authors who are experts in this area abound; many are listed in the References and Further Reading section of this book. Even those who are unaware of differentiation realize that in a classroom of students, there are those who are more advanced learners and those who are far below grade-level expectations. There are students who have a proclivity for the arts and others who have a tendency to favor the sciences. Some students are content sitting for most of the day at a desk, whereas others are clamoring for time to move about the room or school campus. The list of ways that contribute to student diversity is an extensive one. Students are also keenly aware of the fact that there are differences among them. Just as students know that on a given sports team, not all players are experts in every position, so do students realize that their classmates possess a variety of expertise and interest in areas relating to school work and learning styles. Teachers who employ differentiation are aware of student differences and capitalize on opportunities to challenge students to their abilities, taking into account learner interests, readiness, and learning styles. These teachers' mission is to seek out and learn ways to meet their students' needs. In turn, students appreciate teachers who understand and respond to differences.

DEFINITION: CONTENT, PROCESS, PRODUCT

Carol Ann Tomlinson, a leading author in this field, crystallizes the definition of differentiation in this way: "In a differentiated classroom, the teacher proactively plans and carries out varied approaches to content, process, and product in anticipation of and response to student difference in readiness, interest, and learning needs" (Tomlinson, 2001). Below is a cursory definition of the major components of differentiation; throughout the book, specific examples are provided.

Content

The *content* is the essential knowledge, understandings, and skills of a unit of study or lesson. To identify the content, teachers refer to content standards from the district, state, or school in addition to accessing textbooks, curriculum, and other guides and deferring to teacher expertise.

This combination of sources will most likely be needed for teachers to clearly identify the content—what students should know, understand, and be able to do. Some refer to the content as the *input* since teachers are filling up students' brains with new information.

Teachers introduce students to content in a variety of ways. The traditional way is through a textbook or lecture. Other ways include a performance, a video, computer software, a Web site, a field trip, an audiotape, a guest speaker, a summary, an article, and so forth. As teachers come to know their students through formal and informal assessments, they can present content in a differentiated way. For example, content-area teachers can have several biographies available on various individuals and at different levels of readability. The teacher then assigns students appropriate biographies based on students' reading levels and takes into account their interests in a particular noteworthy figure. Or a social studies teacher can arrange students in groups according to their interests on a particular topic, such as a country. Each group then reads various resources centered on the country of choice. Alternatively, the teacher can arrange groups homogeneously by ability and assign more difficult reading to high-achieving students and more accessible text to those who are struggling.

Teachers do not necessarily have to differentiate content for each lesson all the time. They can present the whole class with a resource, such as a video, and then differentiate subsequent activities by instructing groups of students who are arranged by ability level or interest to explore further. For example, if students are studying slavery, a teacher might present an excerpt from a video of Alex Haley's *Roots* to the entire class to expose them to specific content. For further acquisition of this content, the teacher can divide students into readiness-based groups and assign various reading material at an appropriately challenging level for each group. This might mean using a more advanced textbook for the most able readers and providing an excerpt from a grade-level text for other students. Struggling students might be challenged through a brief summary that exposes key ideas.

Process

Process is the method used to make sense of the content. In other words, *process* is the sense-making part of a lesson when teachers call upon students to assimilate and apply the information presented in the content. Typically, this is done through classroom activities and lessons that teachers conduct, although homework assignments are also part of the process.

One frequently used differentiated strategy for teaching or reteaching is through mini-workshops or small-group instruction. In this strategy, students are preassessed to determine their understanding of a particular skill, concept, or topic—for example, their ability to use complex sentences, define *mitosis,* or identify the main idea of a reading selection. Based on this information, teachers might pull a small group of students who need additional support to hone this learning and conduct a mini-workshop to assist them. Or an alternative method is when teachers create and assign several versions of an assignment to appeal to different ability levels. The preassessment will provide information about which assignment is best suited for each student or groups of students. These previous examples highlight differentiation for readiness level, but teachers can also preassess students in terms of learning style or interest and provide assignment choices so students can work within their preferred learning mode or area of interest.

Another common differentiation practice for process is questioning. Teachers can differentiate questions that appeal to students' interests and also that consider students' readiness. In the latter, questions for advanced learners are those that contain more depth and complexity; however, all learners are given questions that address the overarching concepts of a given lesson or unit. Developing various learning centers, journal prompts, lab experiments, and project choices are just some of the many other ways to differentiate for process.

Any activity or lesson that teachers conduct in the process stage constitutes practice so students have the opportunity to use the content and construct clear understandings. Throughout this critical time of teaching, it is prudent to continually assess how well students are doing and adjust lessons or activities as appropriate. Teachers will feel the need to formulate their own system of accountability; however, they should not overgrade these types of assessments as the emphasis is on practice. A tangible formative assessment for an activity might be a journal-writing response, a math-problem-of-the-week write-up, or an outline. A less concrete albeit critical indicator of how students are faring in their understanding is through observing their participation in small-group tasks and whole-group discussion. When teachers consistently and consciously employ formative (or ongoing) assessment throughout the entire course of a unit, they are able to offer learning that best meets students' needs by, for example, pulling small groups to reteach, revising a lesson, or varying the pace of instruction.

Formative assessment yields valuable information about the effectiveness of curriculum and instruction. During lessons and activities (process), teachers rely on formative assessments to get a pulse on students' understanding of a targeted skill or concept. As Douglas Fisher and Nancy Frey (2007) state in *Checking for Understanding: Formative Assessment Techniques for Your Classroom*, the purpose is "to improve instruction and provide student feedback." It gives teachers the ability to redirect and strengthen teaching that can have an immediate impact on learners. Chapter 4 includes a number of formative assessment examples and ideas.

Product

As evidence of learning after a considerable unit of study, teachers then issue a culminating product (or summative assessment) to demonstrate students' understanding of a unit's content and process. Since content is what students should know, understand, and be able to do, the product should be designed in a way that allows students to demonstrate this learning and to do so with clear and appropriate criteria for success. Some teachers issue a test after a given segment of learning, which signifies just one type of product. But products also come in other forms. Teachers should consider issuing both a final exam and a different type of product for a comprehensive assessment of what students have come to know, understand, and be able to do.

In a language arts classroom, products can include a performance, a poster project, an interview, or a formal writing assignment (e.g., response to literature, persuasive, summary). In a science class, a summative assessment could be writing a lab report or building a kite in a physics unit. Differentiating products is a powerful and valuable means of allowing students to exhibit what they have learned. Teachers should present the summative assessment to students at the beginning of the unit so they are well aware of expectations and have specific goals in mind as they work to accomplish each task that leads to the final product.

STUDENT CHARACTERISTICS: READINESS, INTEREST, LEARNING PROFILE

Teachers differentiate content, process, and/or product as they take into account students' readiness, interest, and learning profile. If teachers differentiate by pairing student characteristics with the curriculum and instruction, powerful learning is the result. Teachers can address one or a combination of characteristics, such as readiness and interest, when planning differentiated lessons or units. Following is a brief explanation of these three key types of student characteristics; there are a multitude of resources on each facet presented here, especially on learning profile. The References and Further Reading section provides a partial list of books, but teachers are encouraged to search for their own resources to foster their students' learning in any of these areas.

Readiness

Through pre- and ongoing (or formative) assessments, teachers can glean information regarding what students know, understand, and can do so they can gauge their *readiness*. Readiness varies from student to student, and teachers need to differentiate to appropriately challenge each student at his or her ability level. If students receive material way too demanding for them, they will feel defeated and frustrated. On the other hand, if they are given work that is far below their ability, they are insulted or are turned off completely. Moderately challenging students just above what they are capable of performing is necessary for learning. When teachers differentiate content based on readiness level, they might gather materials across a spectrum of readability and assign students reading selections accordingly. A tiered activity in which teachers modify and extend a particular assignment so that it has various versions at varying levels of difficulty is one example of differentiation by readiness. Other brief examples are given in the list below and throughout this book.

- In a core classroom of language arts/social studies, assign students to read one of three different books that are chosen specifically by readability. The advanced group reads selections by Frederick Douglass, the grade-level group reads *The Slave Dancer* by Paula Fox, and the struggling group reads *Nightjohn* by Gary Paulsen. During the reading, students at all levels from struggling to high achieving complete various tasks individually and in small groups related to the guiding question: *How does the historical setting affect individuals?* As an extension, the high-achieving group might investigate answers to more complex questions, which might require additional reading, such as: *How does social or political oppression lead to conflict or revolution? How do the physical and emotional results of conflict create lasting change for members of society?*

- During a research project, teachers provide a list of topic choices based on the level of difficulty of the topic. Then, teachers assign high-achieving students a list of more sophisticated topics that require more extensive or introspective research.

- In math, assign different math prompts for students to complete that are at various levels of difficulty with high achievers solving more complex problems than struggling students. Students can even create problems for one another to solve.

- Divide science students into groups based on ability levels. Instruct each group to complete one of three lab experiments that are designed to challenge each group appropriately. For students approaching grade level, scaffold the lab so it is accessible to them by providing more concrete directions with examples and adult assistance. Or, expect all students to complete the same lab but provide extension learning opportunities for high achievers, such as posing more challenging problems, creating prediction scenarios, or connecting the work to professions in the world.

Interest

When teachers take into account students' likes and dislikes, they differentiate according to *interest*. Differentiating this way is powerful in that students are more apt to be engaged in learning when it taps into what appeals to them, and there are specific instances where this type of differentiation might apply. Even if a state standard dictates that students write in a particular genre, there still can be the opportunity to consider student interest. For example, students might be expected to write a biography, but teachers can allow each student to choose his or her own subject as the basis for writing. Similarly, teachers who give students the freedom to choose a topic for a persuasive writing assignment from a comprehensive student-generated list or a research topic from a current unit of study are thus engaging in interest-based differentiation. Selecting a novel as the basis of a literature circle or independent reading is another such example.

Learning Profile

Learning profile encompasses a broad range of areas that involve how students learn best. It most commonly includes learning style and intelligence preferences. Teachers who present content in the same way repeatedly to all students and expect the entire class to demonstrate their learning through only written means do not vary learning styles but rather expect students to work in one modality. Conversely, teachers who selectively present content to groups of students through a variety of ways—video, taped recording, reading selection, hands-on experiment, field trip—are conscious of learning profiles. There are several ways to assign activities that are appropriate for students' learning profiles too. And students can choose products in their preferred modality, such as an interview, storyboard, performance, or written composition—one that best suits their learning style and demonstrates their understanding of the concepts and skills presented in a lesson or unit. Teachers know that students do not always operate in the same learning style for all discipline areas.

Rita Dunn and Ken Dunn (1987) developed a widely accepted learning-style model that includes five classifications of learning styles as summarized in Figure 1.1.

Another commonly known learning profile is *multiple intelligences,* which was conceived by Howard Gardner (1983). He identifies eight different ways to demonstrate intellectual ability, as shown in Figure 1.2, along with suggestions for planning differentiated curriculum opportunities.

Equally noteworthy is Robert Sternberg's (1996) model of intelligence that includes three skill areas: analytical, creative, and practical. Analytical intelligence encompasses those skills most taught in school and represents linear thinking. It involves comparing and contrasting, making judgments, and defining cause-and-effect relationships. Creative thinkers are innovators who have original approaches and ideas and are good at problem solving. The practical thinkers are "street smart" and have the need to know why and how things work within a context in the greater world.

Linking Interest- and Readiness-Based Differentiation

Designing differentiated opportunities that address both interest and readiness is a challenging task, with the goal being to maximize learning.

Learning Styles

Learning Style	Description
Auditory learners	Students who are auditory learn best through listening. They prefer listening to a lecture or book rather than receiving the information from reading. They like to engage in discussions so they can talk and listen to their classmates about content, ideas, and opinions. Furthermore, they glean much information from speaking strategies, such as pitch, intonation, pacing, and gestures. To appeal to the learning style of auditory learners, teachers might suggest that these students read text aloud and use a tape recorder.
Visual learners	As the term indicates, visual learners learn best through seeing. This means they prefer to read along when a teacher is reading or will need to display the information they hear visually by taking notes or developing graphic organizers. Teachers can assist visual learners by making sure information that is presented is also shown on PowerPoint slides, transparencies, a document camera, handouts, pictures, or videos so they can better assimilate the information. When someone is presenting, it is important to these students that they are able to see the person talking so they can read facial cues and body language. Therefore, an unobstructed view to the teacher or featured speaker is important.
Tactile learners	Students who are tactile like working with their hands. They learn best through touching, so provide math manipulatives, drawing devices, science apparatus, or other materials that they can use for hands-on learning.
Kinesthetic learners	Kinesthetic learners learn best by being physically active in the learning process. They like doing and moving so they can assimilate and connect the information presented so that it is meaningful to them. These students find it difficult to sit and would rather move around the classroom.
Tactile/kinesthetic learners	Tactile/kinesthetic learners learn through moving, doing, and touching. These students want to be physically involved in a hands-on way. Since they have a need to be active and explore, they cannot sit still for long periods of time. Simulations and role-playing are appropriate strategies for these students.

FIGURE 1.1

There are several ways to connect interest and readiness in any classroom. One such example is the strategy of literature circles (Daniels, 1994) in which students are organized in groups with others who have selected the same reading text. Typically, all the students focus on the same genre (e.g., biography, autobiography, classic literature, or historical fiction), author, or a consistent theme such as alienation, coming of age, or conflict.

Multiple Intelligences

Multiple Intelligence	Summary of Each Intelligence	Differentiated Curriculum Suggestions
Verbal/ linguistic	Reading, writing, listening, speaking	• Use storytelling to . . . • Write a poem, myth, legend, short play, or news article about . . . • Lead a class discussion on . . . • Create a radio program about . . . • Invent slogans for . . . • Conduct an interview of . . . on . . .
Logical/ mathematical	Working with numbers and abstract patterns	• Create story problems for ... • Translate ... into a formula for... • Create a timeline of ... • Invent a strategy game that ... • Make up analogies to explain ...
Visual/spatial	Working with images, mind mapping, visualizing, drawing	• Chart, map, cluster, or graph ... • Create a slide show, videotape, or photo album of ... • Design a poster, bulletin board, or mural of ... • Create advertisements for ... • Vary the size and shape of ... • Color-code the process of ...
Musical/ rhythmic	Using rhythm, melody, patterned sound, song, rap, dance	• Give a presentation with a musical accompaniment on ... • Sing a rap song that explains ... • Indicate the rhythmical patterns in ... • Explain how a piece of music is similar to ... • Use music to enhance learning ... • Create a musical collage to depict ...
Bodily/ kinesthetic	Processing information through touch, movement, dramatics	• Role-play or simulate ... • Choreograph a dance of ... • Invent a board or floor game of ... • Build or construct a ... • Devise a scavenger hunt to ... • Design a product for ...
Interpersonal	Sharing, cooperating, interviewing, relating	• Conduct a meeting to ... • Act out diverse perspectives on ... • Intentionally use ... social skills to learn about ...

FIGURE 1.2 *(Continued)*

Multiple Intelligence	Summary of Each Intelligence	Differentiated Curriculum Suggestions
		• Teach someone else about … • Collaboratively plan rules or procedures to … • Give and receive feedback on …
Intrapersonal	Working alone, self-paced instruction, individualized projects	• Set and pursue a goal to … • Describe how you feel about … • Describe your personal values about … • Write a journal entry on … • Do a project of your choice on … • Self-assess your work in …
Naturalist	Spending time outdoors, sorting, classifying, noticing patterns	• Collect and categorize data on … • Keep a journal of observations about … • Explain how a plant or animal species resembles … • Make a taxonomy of … • Specify the characteristics of … • Attend an outdoor field trip to …

FIGURE 1.2

Source: The multiple intelligence summaries are from *Differentiated Instructional Strategies: One Size Doesn't Fit All,* 2nd edition, by G. Gregory and C. Chapman. Thousand Oaks, CA: Corwin Press, 2007, pp. 33–34. The differentiated curriculum suggestions are from *Multiple Intelligences and Student Achievement: Success Stories From Six Schools* by Bruce Campbell and Linda Campbell. Alexandria, VA: Association for Supervision and Curriculum Development, 1999, p. 69.

Teachers usually conduct literature circles during language arts, but they are certainly suitable for other subject areas too. For example, a social studies teacher can offer a variety of historical fiction as the basis for literature circles, or science teachers can provide a selection of biographies on various scientists.

Each student is responsible for a prescribed role that has specific expectations, and each role is rotated. Daniels (1994) offers a list of roles, although teachers tend to expand on them. For example, one student is the "Discussion Director" whose responsibility it is to generate questions and facilitate a group discussion around these questions. Another student assumes the role of "Capable Connector," sharing and facilitating a conversation about connections with characters and themes in other selections or with the real world. Eventually, students internalize the roles and are able to discuss them in depth without the aid of prescriptive jobs and their directions.

Although it is important in literature circles for students to choose a reading selection from a list of choices that interest them, it is equally important that the text is not too advanced or effortless for each student's reading ability, but rather presents an appropriate challenge. To arrange this proper balance, teachers provide controlled choice by preparing a list of reading selections that represent all different levels of readability. Students choose three books from this list that interest them. Then, teachers review each student's three selections and purposefully assign just the right book for each pupil. A teacher can satisfy the needs of a struggling student who has selected as his first choice a book too challenging by assigning him his third choice, a book more appropriate for his reading level. In this scenario, students read selections of interest to them while the teacher assists with making sure the readability level and content of the texts are appropriately challenging. This combination of interest and readiness can yield meaningful learning opportunities.

Linking Learning Style and Readiness-Based Differentiation

Teachers can also differentiate by linking learning style and readiness. For example, students can choose a culminating project from among a teacher-generated list that addresses their learning style, for example, an interview (for more outgoing students), a short story (for those who like to write), a PowerPoint presentation (for the technology-minded student), a detailed illustration (for the artistically inclined), a musical composition (for the musician), and so forth. To include the element of readiness, teachers can allow students to choose the project type but direct the content. The content on which the project is based could be the result of reading text at different levels of challenge (e.g., articles, textbook chapters, picture books), focusing the project on topics that span levels of difficulty, or analyzing different laboratory outcomes and basing the project on the findings.

DIFFERENTIATED STRATEGY SUGGESTIONS

Figure 1.3 includes several strategies along with suggestions for differentiating instruction. A brief overview and example of how each strategy can be used is included along with identification of content, process, and/or product and whether it applies to readiness, interest, or learning profile. More thorough applications and explanations of some strategies are located throughout this book. With the pervasive nature of this topic, however, one book cannot possibly provide all the necessary information about differentiation. Therefore, refer to the References and Further Reading section for a list of books that serve to improve teachers' awareness, understanding, and implementation of differentiation.

Differentiating Instruction

What Is the Strategy?	How Do I Use It?
Various texts, resources, supplemental materials	*Content for Readiness:* Teachers can make available a wide array of reading materials at various levels of readability, for example, textbook excerpts from different grade-level texts (and not just the text from the current grade taught), supplemental materials from publishers, various articles, pictures books, and so forth. Teachers assign different groups or individuals appropriately challenging text based on students' reading abilities.
	Content for Interest: In a readiness-based situation, students are assigned reading materials that are appropriately challenging. In an interest-based model, students choose the texts, resources, and materials that involve topics of interest to them.
	Process for Readiness: Similar to providing a wide array of reading material for students to acquire content knowledge, teachers can make available a multitude of resource material at varying levels of difficulty so students can process this content. High-achieving students can read materials that are more complex and advanced. Struggling readers will be assigned less complicated material. Additionally, teachers can employ other differentiated strategies for these students, such as reading partners and using classmates' notes to guide or supplement reading.
	Process for Learning Profile: Teachers consider students' learning styles when providing various kinds of resource materials for students to assimilate content, for example, interviews, demonstrations, computer software, videotapes, or reading excerpts.
Organizing ideas through graphic organizers (or other methods)	*Content or Process for Readiness:* As students read various-leveled texts or materials or listen to a lecture, teachers may assign different graphic organizers based on readiness with some more challenging and that ask for more complex understanding than others. Although the organizers vary in design and complexity, all students are expected to acquire conceptual understanding of overarching themes. Teachers might also copy and share completed organizers from students who could benefit from classmates' notes. Teachers can also issue different organizers to students to use as a prewriting tool. These brainstorming sheets are modified or more complex, and each mirrors the differentiated writing rubrics students address.
	Content or Process for Learning Profile: Some students organize information through outlining to better understand and assimilate the information; some students prefer writing a brief summary. Teachers who allow students to choose an organizational method that best suits individual learning styles are assisting students in grasping the information. Besides outlining and summarizing, students might create or select a web, chart, diagram, storyboard, and so forth to organize thoughts in a way suitable for individual learning characteristics. There are many Web sites that feature graphic organizers: · • http://www.eduplace.com/graphicorganizer/ • http://www.edhelper.com/teachers/graphic_organizers.htm • http://www.nvo.com/ecnewletter/graphicorganizers/ • http://www.region15.org/curriculum/graphicorg.html

FIGURE 1.3 (*Continued*)

What Is the Strategy?	How Do I Use It?
Reading buddies or partners/ reciprocal teaching (Palincsar, 1985, 1986)	*Content for Readiness:* Pair students to read material to supplement concepts presented. Students read material silently and then aloud to each other and discuss the material presented. To differentiate by readiness, teachers pair students of comparable reading abilities. Teachers may also choose to employ the reciprocal teaching strategy so partners have a prescribed method of discussing and understanding materials read through predicting, questioning, summarizing, and clarifying, which represent the hallmark of the Reciprocal Teaching strategy.
Varied computer programs	*Content for Readiness:* Just as teachers assign students designated material to read based on students' levels of reading and comprehension, so can teachers assign students to work on a software program geared to a certain level of difficulty matched to each learner.
Tape-recorded materials	*Content for Readiness/Learning Profile:* Some students are better able to assimilate and understand material if they hear it tape-recorded. Allow those students who are struggling readers or those who are highly auditory to listen to tape-recorded material in lieu of reading an excerpt, to follow along with a reading excerpt, or to supplement the reading with an additional tape-recorded piece. Here are some options: • Kurzweil 3000 (www.kurzweiledu.com) is a program designed to help low-performing students and those with some learning disabilities read and write and be independent learners. Students can scan in a teacher's handout or an article, and the Kurzweil will read the article out loud. There are options to read slower or faster, to take notes, and to highlight text. • Microsoft Word has a tape-recording feature that can help students read. • Teachers can also tape-record a lecture and allow students to listen to the lecture again and read a copy of accompanying lecture notes. • If a story is not currently available on tape or CD, invite students who read with strong inflection and modulation to tape-record stories to share with students who could benefit from listening. Students can also download novels onto their iPods from iTunes, but this source is limited. • Recording for the Blind & Dyslexic (RFB&D), a national nonprofit and volunteer organization, has produced accessible educational materials for students with disabilities (e.g., visual impairment or dyslexia) that make reading standard print difficult or impossible. Their digitally recorded textbooks and novels are available in every subject area and grade level from kindergarten through graduate studies. Those interested can become members, and it operates similarly to a lending library (www.rfbd.org). • LibriVox (www.librivox.org) provides free audiobooks from the public domain. Volunteers record chapters of books in the public domain and release the audio files back onto the Net. Their catalog includes more than 1,500 works from which to choose.
Videotapes	*Content for Readiness/Learning Profile:* Assign students to watch videotapes to supplement an explanation or a lecture.

FIGURE 1.3 *(Continued)*

What Is the Strategy?	How Do I Use It?
Visual, auditory, tactile, kinesthetic modes	*Content for Learning Profile:* To maximize learning opportunities for all students, teachers can present content that addresses their varied learning styles. For example, teachers can accompany lectures (auditory) by showing graphic organizers or notes (visual) on an overhead, a document camera, or a PowerPoint slide. Or teachers can set up math stations with manipulatives (tactile) or assign students to act out a part of a play (kinesthetic).
Jigsaw (Aronson, 1978; Clarke, 1994; Clarke, Widerman, & Eadie, 1990; Slavin, 1994)	*Content and Process for Readiness/Interest:* The jigsaw strategy involves groups of students reading different material based on readiness or their interests. Students then teach each other what they have learned. *Group configuration #1:* Students are arranged in initial groups and assigned or choose a subtopic of a greater topic of study. Students read, discuss, and clarify information about the subtopic to become experts. *Group configuration #2:* Students form a different group comprised of one individual from the first group, who have become experts on a subtopic. Each student's job is to teach others in his or her group about what she or he has learned from the first group. Students may ask questions for clarification and take notes on the subtopic a classmate has explained. At the end of the exercise, students will have learned information about several subtopics. *Extension:* Teachers extend the jigsaw with additional activities to further students' understanding of the reading, plus they can issue an assessment.
Curriculum compacting (Reis, Burns, & Renzulli, 1992)	*Content, Process, or Product for Readiness/Interest/Learning Profile:* According to Reis, Burns, and Renzulli (1992), "the term *curriculum compacting* refers to a process in which a teacher preassesses above-average-ability students' skills or knowledge about content prior to instruction and uses this information to modify curriculum." This strategy is used for students who can master information at a faster pace. Although the authors present eight specific steps, there are three basic phases to curriculum compacting: (1) identify learning objectives or standards of the curriculum to be taught; (2) preassess students on what they know, understand, and are able to do in a given unit; and (3) plan and provide curriculum enrichment for students who have mastered learning objectives based on preassessment results. Although readiness drives curriculum compacting, teachers should collaborate with students to consider interest and learning style preferences as well.
Learning contracts (Tomlinson, 2001; Winebrenner, 2001)	*Content, Process, or Product for Readiness/Interest/Learning Profile:* A learning contract is an agreement between the teacher and student about independent work that the student will accomplish with teacher guidance. It can be part of the curriculum compacting plan or not. The contract can take many forms and can be used for individuals or groups of students. For example, a student who has shown mastery of certain skills and concepts from a preassessment can work on a learning contract while the class works on teacher-directed learning. During some lessons, these students work independently on the contract, but other times they join the class for whole-group activities or lessons with content matter they need to learn. Students with learning contracts must abide by working conditions and rules set forth by the teacher and agreed to by the student(s), such as working quietly, not disturbing the teacher when she or he is teaching, following activity directions, maintaining a log of work accomplished, abiding by time lines, etc. Criteria for performance (or scoring guide) are necessary to focus students as they work on projects.

FIGURE 1.3 (*Continued*)

What Is the Strategy?	How Do I Use It?
Learning centers	*Process for Readiness:* Teachers can teach, extend, and reinforce the skills and concepts of a particular unit through learning centers. In this strategy, teachers create several meaningful activities and organize/arrange the materials and directions of these activities throughout the classroom—on the floor, at a back table, on a cluster of desks pulled together. Students are then directed to certain activities—or learning centers—to acquire readiness-based competencies they need to learn. For example, teachers will dictate that some students visit Centers #1 and #2, and go to other centers only if time allows. Other students are designated to visit Centers #3 and #4. Students show evidence of the work completed at each center through a visible recordkeeping device set up in the classroom or by housing work in a folder.
Interest centers	*Process for Interest:* Similar to learning centers, interest centers are set up throughout the classroom or housed in folders or boxes that can be worked on at students' desks. Interest centers are meant to allow students to explore a topic in further depth based on their interests. This interest-based motivation is what differentiates interest centers from learning centers, which focus more on mastery. The topics for interest centers can be related to a current unit of study or another topic outside the unit.
Games to practice mastery of information and skills	*Process for Readiness:* Teachers can arrange for students to play a variety of games to review and master skills and information. Teachers or students can prepare game cards by level of difficulty and assign students to answer selected questions. Teachers can make game cards based on popular games (e.g., Jeopardy, Bingo) or make their own generic game board and create clues based on unit content. Clue and answer cards can be color-coded based on difficulty level. Students can act out differentiated concepts or vocabulary words/terms for others to guess. Instead of creating their own, teachers can find various games at conferences where vendors sell their wares, at teacher supply houses, or by searching online; or they can even alter popular games to meet the needs of students.
Anchor activities	*Process for Readiness/Interest:* Because students work at different paces, in a differentiated classroom students are given a choice of activities (called anchor activities) to work on independently when they finish work early. As students work on these activities that extend the concepts and skills of a lesson or unit, teachers have the opportunity to pull individuals or small groups of students for assessment or further instruction.
Mini-workshops	*Process for Readiness:* To teach or reteach a skill, concept, or topic, teachers can conduct mini-workshops and invite selected students who are in need of honing targeted learning to participate. Through pre- and ongoing assessments, teachers can detect which students are in need of additional instruction. Teachers would then invite those students to attend a mini-workshop on this skill, topic, or concept as an adjunct to whole-group instruction. Other names for mini-workshops are (1) small-group instruction or (2) flexible-skills grouping if the work of the group focuses on skill building only. Teachers can conduct mini-workshops for a small group while others are working on anchor activities.

FIGURE 1.3 (*Continued*)

What Is the Strategy?	How Do I Use It?
Homework assignments	*Process for Readiness:* Teachers assign homework at varying difficulty levels to students based on readiness. Differentiating homework assignments serves to further elucidate and challenge students' understanding of a given concept, skill, or topic. For example, teachers can assign different levels of writing or math prompts; in language arts, teachers can assign short stories at different levels of complexity; in science, teachers can offer different challenge levels of science articles for students to read and summarize.
Multiple levels of questioning (California Department of Education, 1994)	*Process for Readiness:* Questioning is an effective strategy used in classrooms, but in a differentiated classroom specific questions can be purposefully devised to challenge groups of students at varying levels of difficulty and complexity. All questions, though, emanate from the overarching concepts the class is studying. It would behoove teachers to explore the research of Dr. Sandra Kaplan from Southern California's Rossier School of Education when devising differentiated questions. Drawing from her work, key vocabulary is used as the impetus to enrich content knowledge through depth within a discipline and complexity across disciplines. Key words and phrases to foster questioning include *patterns, rules, trends, vocabulary, ethics, traits,* and *purposes.*
Exit cards	*Process for Readiness:* Teachers prepare prompts that they issue to students during the last 3 to 5 minutes of class. The prompts relate to the day's lesson, and students respond to them as a way for teachers to check for understanding and progress and for students to reflect upon key learning. Students can respond on index cards or scraps of paper. Students put their names on their exit cards and the teacher collects them. Afterwards, teachers sort the cards into three piles according to students' understanding: (1) students who are on target and clearly understand what is taught, (2) students who kind of "get it," and (3) students who are clearly floundering and need additional support. With this information, teachers can differentiate instruction by modifying or extending the subsequent lessons. Exit cards can be used on an ongoing basis as part of a teacher's routine, or they can be used on a periodic basis as a teacher deems necessary. Some teachers call exit cards "tickets to leave" since the students hand teachers their cards before leaving the classroom.
Literature circles (Daniels, 1994)	*Process for Readiness/Interest:* Teachers present a collection of books at varying reading levels and topics of interest to students. In groups, students read the same book and are each assigned a specific role that rotates among students. The roles are intended to illuminate the reading by providing a structured way to delve into the complexities of a work of literature. Once students are well versed in the roles, the structured aspect of each job is suspended so spontaneity will emerge. This same model can be used with nonfiction text, as well.
Think-Pair-Share (Lyman, 1981, 1992)	*Process for Readiness/Interest:* To facilitate answering questions and factoring in "wait time," teachers can conduct the Think-Pair-Share (T-P-S) strategy to encourage student participation. To use T-P-S: (1) Teachers pose a thoughtful question, (2) students individually think of or write a response, (3) students pair with another and discuss possible answers, and (4) pairs then share their

FIGURE 1.3 (*Continued*)

What Is the Strategy?	How Do I Use It?
	responses with the whole group and continue with discussion. This strategy can be differentiated in many ways, such as pairing students by readiness or by posing an interest-based question for different groups.
Varied journal prompts	*Process for Readiness/Interest:* Teachers can create a list of prompts to issue throughout a unit of study. Students can respond to those prompts of interest or teachers can assign groups of students specific prompts based on level of complexity. To apply to both interest and readiness, teachers can provide a list of interest-based prompt choices among a span of ability levels.
Group work preferences	*Process or Product for Learning Profile:* Some students work best alone, while others excel within a group. Teachers who allow students to choose to work independently, in pairs, or in small groups on activities or products are differentiating according to students' learning profiles.
WebQuest (Kelly, 2000)	*Process or Product for Readiness/Interest:* A WebQuest is a short- or long-term/individual or small-group project. The model was developed by Bernie Dodge at San Diego State University in February 1995 with early input from SDSU/Pacific Bell Fellow Tom March, the Educational Technology staff at San Diego Unified School District, and waves of participants each summer at the Teach the Teachers Consortium. Its focus is inquiry oriented as students research information on teacher preselected Web sites to investigate a research question. Students read and analyze the resources from the Web sites and produce a product showing evidence of understanding. The nature of the activity or project and the associated Web sites can be differentiated by either readiness or interest level or both.
Independent study	*Process or Product for Interest/Readiness:* In an independent study, students discuss with teachers a topic that forms the basis for a project. The focus can be problem based or an exploration of a topic that is of interest to the student. Both teacher and student collaborate to determine the steps in the process to product completion, time line of each step, the form the product will take, and criteria for success. Independent study is also based on readiness as some students may not be prepared to assume the responsibility of independence in completing the product. Students can work independently, in pairs, or in small groups.
Complex instruction (Cohen, 1994)	*Process or Product for Learning Profile:* Teachers emphasize each student's talents and contributions in a cooperative group by creating and assigning specific challenging and complex learning tasks geared to each student's intellectual strength. A significant goal is for students to appreciate each other's intellectual strengths as they work collaboratively to produce a meaningful product. For example, students work together on creating a fictitious island. Tasks within the project include creating a brochure, drawing a detailed map with a legend, orating the political views of the island, and so on.
RAFT (Santa, 1988)	*Process or Product for Readiness/Interest:* RAFT is an acronym for role, audience, format, and topic. Students work on an assignment that takes into account four components: (1) Role: *From whose point of view is the piece written? What role should the student assume?* (2) Audience: *Who is the audience? Who will see, read,*

FIGURE 1.3 (Continued)

What Is the Strategy?	How Do I Use It?
	or use this? (3) Format: *What is the more effective and meaningful product format to show understanding?* (4) Topic: *What is the topic focus for the product or assignment?* Teachers can differentiate for readiness by making more challenging RAFT choices than others or by interest so students can choose the RAFT that most appeals to them. Examples:

American Revolution

Role	Audience	Format	Topic
George Washington	Mother of wounded soldier	Personal letter	How she feels
King George	Sons of Liberty	Document	Why independence is a bad idea
Patrick Henry	Tories or Neutralists	Propaganda	Why fighting for independence is essential

Money

Role	Audience	Format	Topic
Store owner	Customers	Advertisement	All items 10% or 15% off
Baker	Customers	Window sign	Advertising 35% off on some baked goods and 25% off on others
Restaurant owner	Dining customers who are senior citizens	Discounted menu	Entrees 20% off

What Is the Strategy?	How Do I Use It?
Group investigation (Sharon & Sharon, 1992)	*Process or Product for Interest/Learning Profile:* In groups, students select and explore specific subtopics of interest within a general problem area. Students plan and execute investigation relying on multiple sources as they gather, organize, and analyze the information. Groups present their information in a variety of forms that are appropriate for learning styles; classmates and the teacher evaluate the presentations.
Tiered activities, labs, products (Tomlinson, 1999)	*Process or Product for Readiness:* Teachers create various interesting and thought-provoking versions of an activity or culminating product in a range of difficulty levels. Students are then assigned activities or products at an appropriate level of challenge. Even though they vary in the level of complexity, all tiered work focuses on what all students should know, understand, and be able to do. Students can work in pairs or small groups with learners of similar readiness profiles or work independently. If students work in groups, the number of each group will not necessarily be equal given the ability levels of students in a given classroom. For example, there might be one group of four high achievers and

FIGURE 1.3 (*Continued*)

What Is the Strategy?	How Do I Use It?
	two of struggling students. The rest of the groups are comprised of at-grade-level students. Commonly, activities or products are tiered so that there are three varying levels of complexity, but there can also be two or five levels. *Example:* In a poetry unit, one particular assignment can be tiered in which advanced students identify and analyze a poet's use of metaphor, symbolism, and imagery in a sophisticated and complex published poem; at grade level, students identify and analyze the use of metaphor in a less complex poem; struggling learners find two similes in a poem at an appropriate level for them and discuss in a teacher-led group the purpose of the similes used in the piece.
Tic-tac-toe (variations by Winebrenner, 2001; and Tomlinson, 2001)	*Process or Product for Readiness/Learning Profile:* Teachers create a variety of learning-style product choices (e.g., produce a skit, create a song, write a short story or poem) and place them in a tic-tac-toe grid. Students choose which assignments or products they want to complete so that they win a game of tic-tac-toe. Specifically, students choose three assignments that are in a row horizontally, vertically, or diagonally. Teachers can intentionally design the board to apply to readiness by fashioning tasks in appropriate rows based on level of difficulty. Or teachers can create three different tic-tac-toe boards each geared to an ability level. In this way, the tic-tac-toe boards serve as a tiered product for both learning style and readiness.
Portfolios	*Product for Interest:* Teachers can assign students to collect a sampling of their best work in a portfolio. To guide collection, teachers can make a list of the contents of the portfolios and allow for student choice. Within the portfolio, students write a self-reflection answering such questions as: *Which piece is your favorite and why? Which piece might you revise? Which piece shows your best work? Which piece was the most challenging one and why?*
Grade-level and individual student learning rubrics	*Product for Readiness:* Rubrics, or scoring guides, delineate how students will be assessed or evaluated for a given product. It guides both students and teachers in identifying quality work. Sometimes teachers find or create a rubric that represents the key criteria for assessment. They can create rubrics for the different levels of learners in a classroom being mindful of satisfying standards. Other times, teachers and students collaborate to create a rubric that is appropriately challenging to use as a guide for goal-setting when working on a project. The columns represent performance factors (e.g., emergent or approaching grade level, capable, developing, advanced or numbered 1 to 4, 5, or 6). The rows indicate the criteria being assessed.
I-Search (Joyce & Tallman, 1997; Macrorie, 1988) or research project	*Product for Interest:* In an I-Search paper, students actively engage in the research process by exploring answers to interest-based questions that they generate. The research involves four steps from formulating the research question to representing knowledge gained. For a traditional research paper, students can choose a topic of interest within a greater unit of study.

FIGURE 1.3 *(Continued)*

What Is the Strategy?	How Do I Use It?
Community mentorships to guide product	*Product for Interest:* Teachers can assist students in arranging mentorships with employees in the community to complete a product. For example, students who are working on independent study or an I-Search paper might choose a topic related to the environment. To research information for this product, students can spend time working with environmentalists to better understand what qualifications are required in the job, what problems these employees face, how to participate in an environmental study, and so forth.
Community service projects	*Product for Interest:* Students can determine a need in the community and create a service-learning project that reaches out to the community. This appeals to many students because it allows them to do real-world work in an area of interest. For example, students could start a recycling program at a school, organize a tutoring program to benefit struggling students, visit a senior center regularly and read to the seniors or play games with them, or coach younger children in a sport at a local recreation center that is in need of such a program.
Product format choices	*Product for Readiness/Interest/Learning Profile:* Teachers can allow students to show their understanding of what they have learned by choosing a product to complete from a teacher- or student-generated list of choices. Offering several product choices is important when considering each student's learning profile. For example, teachers can list a variety of choices such as interview, short story, project cube, game board, song, PowerPoint presentation, and so on. To design products for readiness and interest, provide a wide array of topic choices that are more challenging and complex for advanced learners and less so for struggling learners. Ensure that all choices are interesting and thoughtful and also allow students to show evidence of conceptual and "big idea" learning. A criterion (rubric) for performance is necessary to guide students as they work on products.
Modify performance assessments	*Product for Readiness/Learning style:* Teachers can assist students in showing what they have learned through modifications of assessments and teacher support. For example, students who have difficulty showing what they know through a written essay that a teacher issues can be asked to tape-record their responses to the essay questions instead. Or students who have fine-motor issues can keyboard their responses. Other ways to support success include (1) extending the due date of products, (2) providing checkpoints along the way with a calendar for students to track and complete work in chunks, and/or (3) submitting sections of a product and assessing them in pieces.

FIGURE 1.3

SUMMARY

Differentiation does not mean that every single lesson or unit includes a differentiated content, process, and product for each and every student's interest, readiness level, and learning profile. As Carol Tomlinson (1999) states in her book *The Differentiated Classroom: Responding to the Needs of All Learners*: "Teachers may adapt one or more of the curricular elements (content, process, product) based on one or more of the student characteristics (readiness, interest, learning profile) at any point in a lesson or unit."

Teachers will instruct students as a whole class in many points throughout the unit and then find it in alignment with the goals of the unit to divide students into differentiated groups for certain activities. Essentially, differentiation is woven in and out of a unit as appropriate; there is no prescribed way that each lesson or unit is to be conducted every time. And it certainly does not mean giving more work to the high achievers and drill practice to lower-level learners. The way and extent to which teachers differentiate depend on the learning goals and the students. But most importantly, it depends on a teacher's willingness to do what is best in the name of education to service students in the more effective way for growth and enlightenment.

Differentiation can be achieved in many different ways. Two teachers who conduct the same lesson or unit can each effectively employ differentiation, although using different techniques, as long as they are clear-sighted about the goals of a given lesson or unit. When teachers are guided by standards and have a firm understanding of the end in mind, they can devise thoughtful curriculum that accounts for the ability levels, learning styles, and interests of their student-clients. This chapter lists a variety of differentiation opportunities (see recap in Figure 1.4). In the following chapters, teachers will receive specific examples and additional support to make differentiation a reality in their classrooms on a consistent basis.

Differentiating Instruction: Recap

Strategy	Readiness	Interest	Learning Profile
CONTENT			
Various texts, resources, supplemental materials	X	X	
Organizing ideas through graphic organizers	X		X
Reading buddies or partner/reciprocal teaching	X		
Varied computer programs	X		
Tape-recorded materials	X		X
Videotapes	X		X
Visual, auditory, tactile, kinesthetic modes			X
Jigsaw	X	X	
Curriculum compacting	X	X	X
Learning contracts	X	X	X

FIGURE 1.4 (*Continued*)

Strategy	Readiness	Interest	Learning Profile
PROCESS			
Various texts, resources, supplemental materials	X		X
Organizing ideas through graphic organizers (or other methods)	X		X
Jigsaw	X	X	
Curriculum compacting	X	X	X
Learning contracts	X	X	X
Learning centers	X		
Interest centers		X	
Games to practice mastery of information and skills	X		
Anchor activities	X	X	
Mini-workshops	X		
Homework assignments	X		
Multiple levels of questioning	X		
Exit cards	X		
Literature circles	X	X	
Think-Pair-Share	X	X	
Varied journal prompts	X	X	
Group work preferences			X
WebQuests	X	X	
Independent study	X	X	
Complex instruction			X
RAFT	X	X	
Group investigation		X	X
Tiered activities, labs, products	X		
Tic-tac-toe	X		X

FIGURE 1.4 *(Continued)*

Strategy	Readiness	Interest	Learning Profile
PRODUCT			
Curriculum compacting	X	X	X
Learning contracts	X	X	X
Group work preferences			X
WebQuests	X	X	
Independent study	X	X	
Complex instruction			X
RAFT	X	X	
Group investigation		X	X
Tiered activities, labs, products	X		
Tic-tac-toe	X		X
Portfolios		X	
Grade-level and individual student learning rubrics	X		
I-Search or research project		X	
Community mentorships		X	
Community service projects		X	
Product format choices	X	X	X
Modify performance assessments	X		X

FIGURE 1.4

Differentiated Lesson Design

OVERVIEW OF LESSON COMPONENTS

This chapter presents a planning template for creating and executing lesson plans that include essential components of a differentiated lesson to ensure that meaningful, choreographed, and effective learning occurs. Within the lesson template are the tenets of a backward design process. Although backward design is commonly used to design whole units of instruction, it is also implemented for effective lesson planning. Reiterating what Tomlinson and McTighe (2006) wrote: "Deliberate use of backward design for planning courses, units, and *individual lessons* results in more clearly defined goals, more appropriate assessments, and more purposeful teaching."

An effective lesson contains key components that are featured in chapters within this book. Adhering to these elements helps ensure a backward design approach of beginning with the end goals of a lesson firmly in mind while designing curriculum. Read and study the comprehensive differentiated lessons included in this chapter. Throughout this book, each chapter is dedicated to defining and explaining each lesson component presented in the sample lessons and featured in the template in Figure 2.1. The intent is for teachers to use the lesson template and specific lesson examples in this chapter, along with subsequent chapters, as tools to build and/or adapt differentiated lessons related to subject-specific content. Lesson components are described in cursory terms as follows:

Guiding—or Essential—Questions (Lesson Title)

A provocative, conceptually-based question that serves as the focus for a lesson (and unit) is a guiding, also known as an essential, question. All activities, readings, lectures, labs, prompts, simulations, or anything that a teacher designs for a lesson and unit all serve to respond to a guiding question. To this point, the template in Figure 2.1 shows that the lesson title is expressed using a guiding question since the focus of the lesson is to answer the question. Unit questions are broader than a lesson guiding question; hence, they begin with "why" or "how." Lesson guiding questions can begin with any question word and serve to prepare students to answer the overarching unit question by scaffolding learning. An example of a unit question is, *How does the historical setting affect characters?* Examples of associated lesson guiding questions are, *What is the historical setting? Who are the characters? What is the relationship between the setting and characters?* As students perform skills and activities, they realize that their overarching purpose is to fully address the guiding questions (see Chapter 3).

Lesson Overview/Unit Context

At the beginning of each lesson, there is a lesson overview that also includes where this lesson fits into the overall unit. It is merely a courtesy to the reader so she or he knows what to expect in the lesson and the outcomes.

Standards

It is important to identify the state or district content standards that the lesson addresses. Throughout this book, the standards used are from Mid-continent Research for Education and Learning's (McREL) *Content Knowledge: A Compendium of Standards and Benchmarks for K–12 Education* by Robert Marzano and John Kendall (2000; http://www.mcrel.org). McREL is widely known and respected for standards development. Their compendium is a synthesis of standards documents from professional subject-area organizations and selected state standards for 14 content areas. Therefore, they should resonate with all educators and are easily transferable. If you match these standards with ones from your own state or district, they will probably be closely aligned (see Chapter 3). Note: To find standards for your specific state and subject area, Web sites and phone numbers, where applicable, of sources to obtain standards are listed in the References and Further Reading section.

Concepts

Lynn Erickson (2002) defines the term *concept* as "a one- or two-word mental construct that is broad and abstract, timeless, universal, and represents a variety of examples that all share the attributes of the concept." *Transportation, migration, symmetry,* and *conflict* are examples of concepts. Lessons and units should address specific concepts so the learning is more in-depth, meaningful, and long-lived (see Chapter 3).

Skills/Activities

Each lesson is intended to teach skills and conduct activities to achieve the purpose of understanding the targeted guiding question. You'll find "Skills/Activities" in two places on the lesson template, Figure 2.1: at the front of the lesson and under "Lesson Details." At the beginning of the lesson template, I include a bulleted list of skills and activities that are the focus for the lesson, such as the following: *Brainstorm a list of ecosystems. Select and research one ecosystem. Create a food chain/web.* Within "Lesson Details," I go into detail about how to actually teach the lesson; therefore, the bulleted list at the front of the lesson could be optional.

Differentiation Strategies

Like "Skills/Activities," I have "Differentiation Strategies" in two places: a bulleted list with a brief statement at the beginning of the lesson template (Figure 2.1) and elaboration of each strategy and instruction on how to use it under "Lesson Details." Since it is elaborated upon in "Lesson Details," the bulleted list could be optional.

Resources/Materials

Any resource or material that a teacher needs to conduct a lesson should be included in the lesson. Resource examples include a textbook chapter, a video clip, a guest speaker, or a newspaper article. Materials encompass anything beyond the routine binder paper, pen, or markers. Teachers might list butcher paper, cardstock, test tubes, graph paper, student journals, and so forth for materials (see Chapter 5).

Timing

Enter the approximate time configuration of what it will take to conduct the lesson, such as one 45-minute class period (see Chapter 5).

Lesson Details (Skills/Activities, Student Grouping, Teaching and Differentiation Strategies, and Extensions)

Lesson details include the following:

- **Skills/activities:** Each lesson includes a brief statement that begins with a verb describing which skill or activity the students will work on (e.g., *List the steps in solving the math problem* or *Compare/contrast the protagonist and antagonist*). This is followed by the detailed steps necessary for students to acquire this skill or complete the activity. In the lesson template, a list of skills is bulleted up front; the step-by-step details of how to initiate and conduct the lesson are scripted here under "Lesson Details" (see Chapter 5).

- **Student grouping:** For a particular lesson, students can work independently, in pairs, or in small groups. The reason for the grouping may be linked to differentiation; for example, a teacher may want heterogeneous groups to work together to solve a problem or homogeneous groups to work on skills not yet acquired. Or the teacher might arrange groups randomly. In a lesson, it is important to explain the type of group and the reason for this grouping (Chapter 5).

- **Teaching strategies:** "Teaching strategies are the methods teachers use to introduce, explain, demonstrate, model, coach, transfer, or assess in the classroom" (Tomlinson et al., 2002). These teaching strategies are embedded within the specifics of a lesson that teachers conduct (see Chapter 5).

- **Differentiation strategies:** Within the step-by-step details of how a lesson is taught, differentiation ideas are highlighted and explained. In the lesson template, a list of differentiation strategies is bulleted up front; the specifics of how to differentiate the lesson along with necessary student handouts are scripted under "Lesson Details." (See various chapters for differentiation ideas.)

- **Extensions:** Teachers might provide students with an opportunity to extend their interest in or knowledge of a unit of study by allowing them to explore related topics or concepts further. This could be individually, in pairs, or in small groups (see Chapter 5).

Assessments

Teachers assess how well students are acquiring knowledge and understanding through pre-, formative (or ongoing), and summative (culminating) assessments. Effective teachers design a variety of assessments through the course of a lesson and unit (see Chapter 4).

COMPREHENSIVE DIFFERENTIATED LESSON SAMPLES

The following lessons are included in this chapter. All teachers can find value in skimming through them to glean differentiation strategies and see how lessons can be constructed even if the subject matter of a lesson is not geared to your teaching assignment.

1. *What are the types, purposes, and audiences for narrative and expository writing?* Initially, I wrote this lesson for a group of science teachers who had the problem of students lacking skills in writing exposition. They felt that their students were so mired in narration that when they came to crafting a science lab write-up, they failed miserably because the language was too flowery. Since then, teachers of various disciplines have conducted this lesson to assist students in preparation for a state or district writing prompt in which students

might be asked to write in either genre, to understand that genres have different purposes and audiences, or to make a clear distinction between the genres as an introduction for an upcoming writing unit in narration or exposition.

2. *How does the author's use of imagery affect the setting?* This lesson is popular among language arts teachers and those who teach a social studies/language arts core or integrate these two subjects. It focuses on students seeing that imagery is a powerful form of figurative language in painting a vivid setting. Students study the use of imagery in authors' works and then translate their knowledge to create a piece of their own.

3. *How do organisms interact and depend on one another through food chains or food webs in an ecosystem?* This is clearly a lesson for science teachers who focus on life sciences, particularly the ecosystem. Students first research an ecosystem and create a food chain or food web showing the interrelationships of organisms within that ecosystem. Then they create a project that shows the effect of the absence of an organism from an ecosystem.

4. *How can I construct a logical argument to justify my reasoning and conclusions?* Math teachers who focus on students using logical arguments as justifications will find value in this lesson that uses pyramid schemes to teach exponents.

Lesson Template

GUIDING—OR ESSENTIAL—QUESTION
(lesson title)

LESSON OVERVIEW/UNIT CONTEXT:

STANDARDS:

CONCEPTS:

SKILLS/ACTIVITIES (cursory, bulleted list only; step-by-step delineated in Lesson Details):

DIFFERENTIATION STRATEGIES (cursory, bulleted list only; step-by-step delineated in Lesson Details):

FIGURE 2.1 *(Continued)*

RESOURCES/MATERIALS:

TIMING (identify how many class periods and length of each class):

LESSON DETAILS (step-by-step explanation of how to conduct lesson; includes skills/ activities students perform or demonstrate, student grouping, teaching strategies, differentiation, extensions):

ASSESSMENTS (list what teachers will use to assess understanding):

FIGURE 2.1

DIFFERENTIATED LESSON SAMPLE #1

GUIDING—or ESSENTIAL—QUESTION

What are the types, purposes, and audiences for narrative and expository writing?

LESSON OVERVIEW/UNIT CONTEXT

In this lesson, students distinguish between exposition and narration by writing and reading examples in each genre and determining the purposes and audiences for each. Any subject-area teacher can conduct this lesson whose goal it is to have students discern expository from narrative writing and focus writing on one or the other depending on the goals of a given unit. This lesson is particularly helpful for science and social studies teachers who have the problem of students leaning toward narrative writing when they expect exposition for various assignments (e.g., lab write-ups, newspaper accounts, research papers, persuasive composition, etc.).

STANDARDS

McREL Standard 1

Uses general skills and strategies of the writing process

- *Benchmark 5:* Uses content, style, and structure (e.g., formal or informal language, genre, organization) appropriate for specific audiences (e.g., public, private) and purposes (e.g., to entertain, to influence, to inform)

McREL Standard 6

Uses reading skills and strategies to understand and interpret a variety of literary texts

- *Benchmark 2:* Knows the defining characteristics of a variety of literary forms and genres (e.g., fiction, nonfiction)

Standard 7

Uses reading skills and strategies to understand and interpret a variety of informational texts

- *Benchmark 2:* Knows the defining characteristics of a variety of informational texts (e.g., textbooks; essays)

CONCEPTS

Exposition, narration, audience, purpose

SKILLS/ACTIVITIES

- Define and discern the differences between narrative and expository writing.
- Determine the purposes and audiences for narrative and expository text.
- Find and write examples of narrative and expository text.

DIFFERENTIATION STRATEGIES

- *Learning style:* Allow students to work individually or in pairs; choose writing type (expository or narrative).

- *Readiness:* Varying levels of text readability; adult assistance; mini-workshop for struggling students; exit cards.

- *Interest:* Choose a picture or object.

RESOURCES/MATERIALS

- "Writing Types" (Figure 2.2)

- "Checking for Understanding" (Figure 2.3)

- "Narrative/Expository Description" (Figure 2.4)

TIMING

Two class periods (based on 43- to 50-minute class periods)

LESSON DETAILS

Class Period #1

1. *Define narrative and expository writing.*

   - Copy and distribute "Writing Types" (Figure 2.2), which includes a writing example of narration and exposition. Instruct students to read each passage and answer the questions listed on the sheet: *What is the name of the genre for this type of writing? What is the author's purpose for this piece? What clues help you to determine the purpose? Who is the author's intended audience?* Tell students they may not be able to answer all the questions, but as a class they will.

     ▶ *Differentiated by learning style:* Allow students to work in pairs or individually on this assignment as they choose.

     ▶ *Differentiated by readiness:* Teachers can tier this assignment by preparing an alternative sheet to the one I have provided for struggling readers. This sheet might include easier text excerpts. Another way to differentiate by readiness is to have an adult partner with a struggling reader to read the text and assist with answering the questions.

   - When individuals or pairs are finished, invite students to share their answers and discuss as a class. During discussion, reveal the names of the genres: narration or narrative writing and exposition or expository writing. Ask them to cite specific reading they have done in various classes or outside of school that fall under each category. For example, a novel you have read in class falls under the narrative genre, and a chapter in a science textbook is an example of expository writing. Arrive at a class definition of each type of writing.

2. *Determine the purposes and audiences for narrative and expository writing.*

   - Ask students: *What are the purposes and audiences for each type of genre?* To do this, have students brainstorm a list of the types of narrative writing, such as short story, novel, personal narrative, memoir, diary entry, and so forth. Then, determine the purpose and audience for each narrative piece (e.g., to entertain, to describe). Do the same for expository. Ask students to list the different expository types of reading/writing, such as research paper, how-to essay, business letter, newspaper article, technical document, and so forth. Have students identify the purposes (e.g., to inform, to explain) and audiences of each type of expository writing listed.

- Return to the "Writing Types" sheet. Now that students have discussed more thoroughly purposes and audiences, allow them to make changes to their answers from the initial discussion.

3. *Find narrative and expository examples.*

- Instruct students to find examples of narrative and expository writing. Make available several types of resources: magazines, textbooks, novels, and so forth. Invite students to use any resource in the classroom (or in the library). They are to share the excerpts with the class. As each student presents an excerpt, his or her classmates (a) determine the type of writing, and (b) identify the purpose and audience from each example. Option: This can also be a homework assignment.

  ▶ *Differentiated by readiness:* Help struggling students by providing them with expository and narrative text that they can have access to and for which they can more easily discern the purpose and audience. Assist them to prepare for the class component when they share with peers.

4. *Discern narrative from expository writing.*

- Conduct an informal checking for understanding to ascertain whether or not students can discern narrative from expository writing. This type of informal ongoing assessment relies on students to use finger symbols to show what they do or do not know to inform teachers immediately of student progress. See Figure 2.3 for the prompts and finger symbol key, but read Figure 4.8 instructions on how to conduct this type of assessment. (This active participation strategy can be used for pre- or ongoing assessments.) Answers are in parentheses after each prompt with an *N* for narrative and an *E* for expository.

  ▶ *Differentiated by readiness:* Pay close attention to student responses. Take note of those students who are still unclear about the differences between expository and narrative. Conduct a mini-workshop with these students who need additional support while others work on an anchor activity. An anchor activity could be responding to a journal prompt or reading an independent book or article.

Class Period #2

5. *Write narrative and expository excerpts.*

- In this exercise, students partner up to each write a paragraph following the rules of either narrative or expository writing based on one picture or object they select. Figure 2.4 is a student handout explaining the assignment; copy and distribute it. Find a variety of pictures or objects from clip art on the computer, from the Web site www.artchive.com, pictures from calendars, or other sources. Find pairs of pictures so students can choose one, such as a beach scene and a wintry forest, or fire and a glacier or ice.

- To help students choose a partner, ask those students who prefer to write expository to raise their hands. Then tell them to partner up with someone whose hand is not raised because these students prefer narrative writing. The reality is that it is unlikely that half the students will raise their hands because they like expository and the other half prefers narrative writing, but have students pair up as best they can.

> ▶ *Differentiated by learning style:* Students choose their own style of writing: narrative or expository.

> ▶ *Differentiated by readiness:* Encourage high-achieving students to write both narrative and expository pieces for a selected picture or object. Or have them work with a peer who is a strong writer and they each write a narrative *and* expository paper for the same picture and compare their writing.

- After students write their pieces, solicit volunteers to read what they wrote. Have classmates determine if the piece is expository or narrative along with the evidence to support their assertions. It is intriguing to compare writing based on the same picture using the same or different genres.

- Have students write a response to the guiding question, *How does narrative writing differ from expository writing?* on an exit card. In Chapter 4, read the explanation for how to issue exit cards under Figure 4.22, "Exit Cards." Teachers have students respond to a prompt on an index card or scrap of paper during the last 3 to 5 minutes of class. Teachers review the responses and determine who needs additional support to grasp the concept or skill and who firmly understands it.

Extensions

- Ask students to return to any papers they have previously written and carefully critique the formality or informality of the language to see if it's suitable for the paper's purpose. They might find that they should have been more mindful of writing in a more expository fashion than narrative or vice versa. Invite them to rewrite their papers armed with the knowledge of the clear distinction between the genres.

- Ask students to create a manual for peers that includes tips for writing in either narrative or expository.

ASSESSMENTS

(This is a recap of assessments throughout the lesson to show formal and informal evidence of student performance.)

- "Writing Types" (Figure 2.2) and observation during discussion
- Published examples of narrative and expository text
- Observation during checking for understanding informal assessment (Figure 2.3)
- Student writing examples of expository or narrative text
- Exit cards
- Paper rewrite (extension)
- Manual (extension)

Writing Types

A: As I finished my second lap, I could feel a stream of sweat dripping down my face. I tried to control my cramp, but it wasn't working so I started sprinting around the azure line that framed the track despite the pain. I could feel my heart beating faster than it had been on my first lap. My curly brown hair flew in a gesture that caught the light of the sun. The jeans I rolled up starting unraveling, and as I ran, the scented spring flowers I smelled turned into a swirl of a magnificent painting by da Vinci. I started feeling dizzy and boiled like a sizzled egg. The thumping of my feet went faster because I was almost finished. My partner Diane cheered like a broken siren, which helped to urge me ahead even though I was not feeling at my best.	What is the name of the genre for this type of writing?
	What is the author's purpose for this piece? What clues help you to determine the purpose?
	Who is the author's intended audience?
B: Physical fitness plays a central role in the readiness of the armed forces. In the United States, several branches of the military formalized the requirement for physical fitness, and developed criteria for measuring strength and endurance. In every model, running stands as the exercise of choice for developing and measuring endurance. In the late sixties, Dr. Kenneth Cooper — a U.S. Air Force lieutenant colonel and flight surgeon — developed the scientific link between aerobic activity and cardiovascular health. His book *Aerobics* and his 12-minute aerobic test for airman gained rapid acceptance among civilian and military communities around the world, and gave birth to the running boom of the seventies.	What is the name of the genre for this type of writing?
	What is the author's purpose for this piece? What clues help you to determine the purpose?
	Who is the author's intended audience?

FIGURE 2.2

Source for A: Kimberly Glass.

Source for B: "Keeping Defenses Strong" by Dr. Kamal Jabbour.

Checking for Understanding

1 - Narrative   2 - Expository
Fist - "I am not sure."

A. Jack London teaches about courage and perseverance in his novella *Call of the Wild,* a heartwarming story about a man's best friend. **(E)**

B. Pool toys drifted in the azure water waiting for children to play with them. The flowers behind the pool were in full blossom, and they smelled sweet as nectar. **(N)**

C. Harriet Beecher Stowe was born into an enormous family of eleven siblings on June 14, 1811, in Litchfield, Connecticut. She died two years after her husband died on July 1, 1896, in Hartford, Connecticut. **(E)**

D. In 1933, the price of stock on the New York Stock Exchange was less than a fifth of what it had been before in 1929. Approximately one out of every four Americans was unemployed in 1932. **(E)**

E. After a game of basketball, we all sat in a pear-shaped circle and played Truth or Dare. When it came to my turn, the boy in the yellow trousers dared me to hit the black car with a bat. Everyone's jaw dropped in a quick snap and no one believed I would actually take the chance. **(N)**

F. In *Righteous Warriors,* the author Meredith Campbell states, "Historical-fiction is that genre of literature that weaves a fictionalized human story around and through actual historical events and eras." **(E)**

G. Leonardo da Vinci was an extraordinary man of many talents who lived during the Renaissance time period. Although he is most known for his artwork, da Vinci was also an inventor and scientist. **(E)**

H. Correcting negative talking is the main idea of Susan Pedwell's article, "How to Turn Off Negative Self-Talk." She presents six steps to correct this behavior. For example, the first step she presents includes that you should tune in to your self-talk throughout the day. **(E)**

I. My cousin, Leo, screeches with enthusiasm and yells down hallways. Sometimes the stench of his clothes overpowers me, and I grimace in disgust. Ebony dirt marks line his face like stripes placed on a zebra. His baggy pants seem as if they are too big for his scrawny waist. While he plays basketball with his 6-year-old friends, his dirty-blond hair blows in the wind like a loose paper dancing in a breeze. **(N)**

FIGURE 2.3

Narrative/Expository Description

Describe an Object or Picture

1. Determine if you like to write in a narrative or expository style. Then, find a partner who prefers to write in a different style than you. Assign A to the person who prefers narrative and B to the expository writer.

2. Together, study the objects or pictures your teacher has shown you. Agree on one object or picture that interests you both.

3. Each of you will write one paragraph based on the same picture without showing each other.

   - *Partner A* describes the object/picture for a **narrative** piece of writing and determines the purpose and audience. Partner A follows these directions: Pretend you are asked to write a plaque based on the picture you and your partner selected. Write this paragraph using proper format for expository writing and be mindful of factual and accurate terms.

   - *Partner B* describes the object/picture for an **expository** piece of writing and determines the purpose and audience. Partner B follows these directions: Write a descriptive paragraph describing the picture you and your partner selected. Pretend your paragraph is a setting for a narrative story, so use sensory detail and figurative language.

4. When finished, be ready to share your paragraphs.

FIGURE 2.4

DIFFERENTIATED LESSON SAMPLE #2

GUIDING—or ESSENTIAL—QUESTION

How does the author's use of imagery affect the setting?

LESSON OVERVIEW/UNIT CONTEXT

In this lesson, students define *imagery* and then identify sensory words and phrases that describe various settings in literature and articulate its effect. As a lesson assessment, students write their own descriptive settings using imagery. This exercise is part of a narrative novel study in which students explore the five elements of literature—setting, plot, character, point of view, and theme.

STANDARDS

McREL Writing Standard 2

Uses the stylistic and rhetorical aspects of writing

- *Benchmark 1:* Uses descriptive language that clarifies and enhances ideas (e.g., establishes tone and mood, uses figurative language, uses sensory images and comparisons, uses a thesaurus to choose effective wording)

McREL Reading Standard 6

Uses reading skills and strategies to understand and interpret a variety of literary texts

- *Benchmark 6:* Understands the use of language in literary works to convey mood, images, and meaning (e.g., dialect; dialogue; symbolism; irony; rhyme; voice; tone; sound; alliteration; assonance; consonance; onomatopoeia; figurative language such as similes, metaphors, personification, hyperbole, allusion; sentence structure; punctuation)

CONCEPTS

Imagery, figurative language, setting

SKILLS/ACTIVITIES

- Identify and provide rationale for a descriptive writing example.
- Determine specific examples of imagery in text excerpt.
- Notice imagery in a novel's settings and evaluate its use.
- Write historical (or any) setting using imagery.
- Revise writing.

DIFFERENTIATION STRATEGIES

- *Readiness:* Tiered reading excerpts; provide word bank and partially completed graphic organizer for struggling students; red/yellow/green strategy for immediate feedback on progress; modify rubric; extend expectations for students to write more than a paragraph.

- *Learning style:* Select picture as a visual guide for writing.
- *Interest:* Choose type of setting as focus for writing.

RESOURCES/MATERIALS

- "Which Setting Is More Descriptive: A or B?" (Figure 2.5)
- "Sensory Details"—3 versions: ♥ approaching-grade-level students; ♣ at-grade-level students; ♠ high-achieving students (Figures 2.6 ♥, 2.7 ♣, 2.8 ♠)
- "Imagery for Setting" (Figure 2.9)
- "Setting Excerpt" (Figure 2.10)
- "Descriptive Setting Checklist" (Figure 2.11)
- "Revision Sheet: Descriptive Setting" (Figure 2.12)
- "Setting Rubric" (Figure 2.13)
- "Setting Rubric Recording Sheet" (Figure 2.14)
- "The 4-6-8-10 Rule" (Figure 2.15)

TIMING

Two class periods (based on 43- to 50-minute class periods)

LESSON DETAILS

Class Period #1

1. *Identify descriptive writing sample and provide support.*

   - Make an overhead of the sheet titled "Which Setting Is More Descriptive: A or B?" (Figure 2.5) or show it with a document camera or SMARTboard. Read the two examples on this sheet and ask students which one is more descriptive. Example A is an excerpt from the novel *When the Emperor Was Divine* by Julie Otsuka and is the more descriptive setting of the two. Ask them to defend their responses using specific words and phrases from the excerpt that explain why the setting they chose is stronger than the other. As an option, replace A or B with an excerpt from literature you are currently reading in class.

2. *Determine specific examples of imagery in text excerpt.*

   - Ask students to name the five senses (sight, sound, smell, taste, touch). Define *imagery:* using sensory words and phrases to paint pictures in a reader's mind so she or he can vividly imagine what is written. Tell students that Example A includes imagery; therefore, it is more descriptive. Revisit their responses about this excerpt and reinforce that imagery was a factor in selecting it.

   - Copy and distribute one of three versions of "Sensory Details" to students based on their ability levels. Each sheet asks students to read a text excerpt and specifically determine which words and phrases are strong examples of imagery. Corresponding to each example, they identify the accompanying sense. For instance, students might highlight "late afternoon sun bathed the cobblestones" and write *sight* as the accompanying sense. Use excerpts taken from literature the students are currently reading instead of the ones I have provided to link it to their current reading.

▸ *Differentiated by readiness:* Use Figure 2.6 with the ♥ symbol for approaching-grade-level students (*Quake!* excerpt); Figure 2.7 with the ♣ symbol for students at grade level ("The Treasure of Lemon Brown" excerpt); Figure 2.8 with the ♠ for high achievers (*Roll of Thunder, Hear My Cry* excerpt). For Figure 2.8, provide and example of imagery in the text that students can use as a guide. To do so, underline sensory words and phrases in the first few sentences and identify the corresponding senses.

- Foster discussion by asking the following questions: *Which words and phrases from the excerpts are strong examples of imagery? Why do authors use imagery in their writing? How does it affect the writing?*

3. *Notice imagery in a novel's settings and record examples.*

- Tell students that they will track examples of imagery in the upcoming novel or selection throughout the duration of the reading. Distribute the sheet titled "Imagery for Setting" (Figure 2.9) to each student. Or students can make their own graphic organizer using the Inspiration notetaking program or even freehand. Explain that when authors feature a setting in the novel or reading, they are to fill in a sheet. One "Imagery for Setting" graphic organizer can be dedicated to a specific setting, or students can compile all examples of imagery onto one or more graphic organizers. Make extra copies of this handout and place the stack somewhere in your classroom so that students have access to it.

- Instruct students to follow these guidelines for completing their imagery sheets: (1) Students identify the settings as they read the novel and stop to record imagery on the graphic organizer(s). (2) Enter words and phrases the author uses verbatim to describe a specific setting with imagery. A phrase is anything more than a word. They are to use quotation marks to indicate these are words and phrases taken directly from the book. (3) If students feel the author could have added imagery to describe a specific setting, students can (and are encouraged to) also enter words and phrases that they feel augment the author's description of a setting. These student additions are not to be in quotes.

  ▸ *Differentiated by readiness:* For struggling learners, pinpoint the particular settings in the selected reading and choose easier setting excerpts. You can also prepare "Imagery for Setting" for each setting by filling in some words and phrases for students, asking them to focus on a few senses and not all five, and providing them with a word bank to use. For more advanced learners, specifically encourage them to add their own sensory details to augment those of the author.

  ▸ *Differentiated by learning style:* Students can create their own graphic organizers on Inspiration 8 software (www.inspiration.com), or select one from a Web site in lieu of using Figure 2.9:

    http://www.eduplace.com/graphicorganizer/

    http://www.edhelper.com/teachers/graphic_organizers.htm

    http://www.nvo.com/ecnewletter/graphicorganizers/

    http://www.region15.org/curriculum/graphicorg.html

- Before students begin to work independently, model this ongoing assignment with them by reading aloud the excerpt from *Johnny Tremain* shown in "Setting Excerpt" (Figure 2.10) or a literary passage your class is currently reading. Make an overhead of this sheet or put it under a document camera or on a SMARTboard, plus distribute a copy to each student so those who are more visually inclined can see it close up as you read.

Note: Mention to students how the paragraphs in the *Johnny Tremain* excerpt are punctuated when multiple paragraphs are quoted—quotation marks are at the *beginning* of each paragraph, but *only at the end* of the entire excerpt.

- Working in pairs, have students reread the *Johnny Tremain* excerpt and complete "Imagery for Setting" (Figure 2.9) using this passage.

  ▶ *Differentiated by readiness:* In Chapter 4, Figure 4.23 features a method of immediately getting feedback of how well students understand a task that teachers have just presented. Read the instructions in detail in Chapter 4. In short, students show one of three color-coded cups or paper strips that indicates their level of understanding. Green indicates that they understand the task at hand and can work independently; yellow indicates they have some questions but can start work and wait for teacher assistance; red means they cannot move forward without the teacher providing guidance. Use this method at this juncture to ascertain how students are faring in this given task. Work with those students who are in need of one-on-one or small-group support.

4. *Debrief the exercise.*

- Ask pairs to contribute what they wrote on their graphic organizers while the teacher records entries for the class to see. Conduct a discussion about what students share using the guiding questions to facilitate discussion: *Which words and phrases from the excerpts are strong examples of imagery? Why do authors use imagery in their writing? How does it affect the writing?* Since this excerpt is historical fiction, continue discussion with this guiding question: *How does imagery impact the historical setting?*

Class Period #2

5. *Write a historical setting using imagery.*

- As a final lesson assessment, students create their own paragraph (or more) of setting to complement literature that teachers are currently reading in their classrooms. This assignment calls for students to write a historical setting using the historical framework they have learned through reading about this time period and also to expand on the events in the novel. This exercise serves a dual purpose of checking for understanding about the novel and writing imagery. It could be easily adapted for any setting as long as students employ imagery. Teachers can have students write a setting with imagery specifically for a short story that students will craft. See the third bulleted item under "Extensions."

- Review the "Descriptive Setting Checklist" (Figure 2.11) with students so they are clear on the writing assignment. Also share the "Setting Rubric" (Figure 2.13) to show the variance between scores and how they will be assessed.

- Then, instruct students to complete the "Imagery for Setting" that they previously used as a reading tool. Encourage them to use selected sensory words and phrases they recorded on this graphic organizer throughout their reading to enhance their use of imagery. Caution students not to overuse the author's words, but rather add to their writing with some of the author's specific sensory words and phrases and rely on their own creations.

  ▶ *Differentiated by interest/learning style:* Allow students to choose a setting for this writing assignment. Provide students with detailed pictures of historical or other settings to use as a guide for writing.

▸ *Differentiated by readiness:* For struggling learners, use one or more of these modifications: (1) Provide students with a list of sensory words and phrases that they can use to write their historical settings or write these words on the "Imagery for Setting" brainstorming sheet. (2) Assist them in choosing a historical or other setting as the topic for writing. (3) Select specific line items on the rubric to focus on for assessment instead of the entire rubric. Assign high achievers to extend the setting into a multiparagraph piece or create a series of descriptive paragraphs focusing on a variety of places.

6. *Revise the writing.*

   - Once finished with their first drafts, students self-assess by filling in the "Revision Sheet: Descriptive Setting" (Figure 2.12) and revise their papers according to their findings on this revision sheet. Both writer and reviewer use the same revision sheet, so make a double set of copies for the class. Let students know that they, as well as a peer, will be completing this revision sheet. This will encourage students to have accountability to write and revise to reflect their personal best. Students revise again based on peer review. Teachers should also provide input on student work.

   - Collect papers and score them against the "Setting Rubric" (Figure 2.13). Record their scores on the "Setting Rubric Recording Sheet" (Figure 2.14), and write any salient comments in the black spaces. These comments can be taken directly from the rubric since it includes specific feedback. Teachers may choose to convert the scores into a letter grade. If so, they can follow the formula on the "The 4-6-8-10 Rule" sheet (Figure 2.15) that Vicki Spandel (2001) devised and features in her book *Creating Writers Through 6-Trait Writing Assessment and Instruction,* 3rd edition.

Extensions

   - Have students identify setting that uses imagery in their independent reading books and answer the guiding question. If their books lack imagery, ask them to rewrite settings that the author could have included that are replete with imagery.

   - Students find magazine or calendar pictures of detailed settings and write a paragraph with imagery to describe the scene. Display all the pictures at a front table and collect the paragraphs separately. Have students match the pictures with the imagery paragraphs. Evaluate which paragraphs utilize strong imagery in a way that describes the picture aptly and those that can be revised to include more.

   - Ask students to write a short story being mindful to include imagery for setting and even characters and events. This extension opportunity can be the culminating unit project in which students write a short story. This setting lesson could then serve as one of a series of lessons in a greater narrative unit.

ASSESSMENTS

(This is a recap of assessments throughout the lesson to show formal and informal evidence of student performance.)

   - Observations of participation in discussions
   - "Sensory Details"—3 versions: ♥ approaching-grade-level students; ♣ at-grade-level students; ♠ high-achieving students (Figures 2.6 ♥, 2.7 ♣, 2.8 ♠)

- "Imagery for Setting" (Figure 2.9): Assess on accuracy, selection of author's words and phrases, and the content of their own words and phrases. Assess both the pair work completed during modeling and also the individual sheets students will complete throughout the reading of the novel.

- "Revision Sheet: Descriptive Setting" (Figure 2.12)

- Historical or other setting with imagery; use rubric to score writing

- Identification of setting with imagery in independent reading books or student writing infused with imagery from book (extension)

- Imagery writing to match picture (extension)

- Short story with imagery for setting, characters, events (extension)

Which Setting Is More Descriptive: A or B?

All through October the days were still warm, like summer, but at night the mercury dropped and in the morning the sagebrush was sometimes covered with frost. Twice in one week there were dust storms. The sky turned suddenly gray and then a hot wind came screaming across the desert, churning up everything in its path. From inside the barracks the boy could not see the sun or the moon or even the next row of barracks on the other side of the gravel path. All he could see was dust. The wind rattled the windows and doors and the dust seeped like smoke through the cracks in the roof and at night he slept with a wet handkerchief over his mouth to keep out the smell. In the morning, when he woke, the wet handkerchief was dry and in his mouth there was the gritty taste of chalk.

B

When I walked outside, I saw a lot of white snow. I expected it to be cold, and it was. The snowman still was standing. I thought that maybe the snow would melt in the afternoon and I could stay outside longer since it might not be so cold. But I wouldn't know for sure until the afternoon would come. In the meantime, I would go to school and stare out the window at the many winter sights wishing I could be rolling in the snow and throwing snowballs at friends. Maybe school will go quickly and the teacher will plan something fun for us all to do.

FIGURE 2.5

♥ Sensory Details ♥

Highlight or underline sensory details from the text.	Write down the senses that reflect what you highlighted or underlined.
At first he didn't notice the dog. Late afternoon sun bathed the cobblestones as Jacob Kaufman trudged up Washington Street to finish the deliveries from his father's meat stand. On such an unusually warm April day, the bustling streets of downtown San Francisco should have been a delight for a boy of thirteen. But since his mother's death, Jacob hardly noticed his surroundings. His mind was blanketed by troubling thoughts, like the fog that sometimes blew in from the bay and blocked out the sun.	

FIGURE 2.6

Source: From *Quake!* by Gail Langer Karwoski (2006), p. 1.

♣ Sensory Details ♣

Highlight or underline sensory details from the text.	Write down the senses that reflect what you highlighted or underlined.
The inside of the building was dark except for the dim light that filtered through the dirty windows from the streetlamps. There was a room a few feet from the door, and from where he stood at the entrance, Greg could see a squarish patch of light on the floor. He entered the room, frowning at the musty smell. It was a large room that might have been someone's parlor at one time. Squinting, Greg could see an old table on its side against one wall, what looked like a pile of rags or a torn mattress in the corner, and a couch, with one side broken, in front of the window.	

FIGURE 2.7

Source: From "The Treasure of Lemon Brown" by W. D. Myers (2002).

♠ Sensory Details ♠

Highlight or underline sensory details from the text.	Write down the senses that reflect what you highlighted or underlined.
By the dawn, the house smelled of Sunday: chicken frying, bacon sizzling, and smoke sausages baking. By evening, it reeked of Christmas. In the kitchen sweet-potato pies, egg-custard pieces, and rich butter pound cakes cooled; a gigantic coon which Mr. Morrison, Uncle Hammer, and Stacey had secured in a night's hunt baked in a sea of onions, garlic, and fat orange yellow yams; and a choice sugar-cured ham brought from the smokehouse awaited its turn in the oven. In the heat of the house, where we had gathered after supper, freshly cut branches of long-needled pines lay over the fireplace mantle adorned by winding vines of winter holly and bright red Christmas berries. And in the fireplace itself, in a black pan set on a high wire rack, peanuts roasted over the hickory fire as the waving light of day swiftly deepened into a fine velvet night speckled with white forerunners of a coming snow, and the warm sound of husky voices and rising laughter mingled in tales of sorrow and happiness of days past but not forgotten.	

FIGURE 2.8

Source: From *Roll of Thunder, Hear My Cry* by Mildred D. Taylor (1997), p. 110.

Imagery for Setting

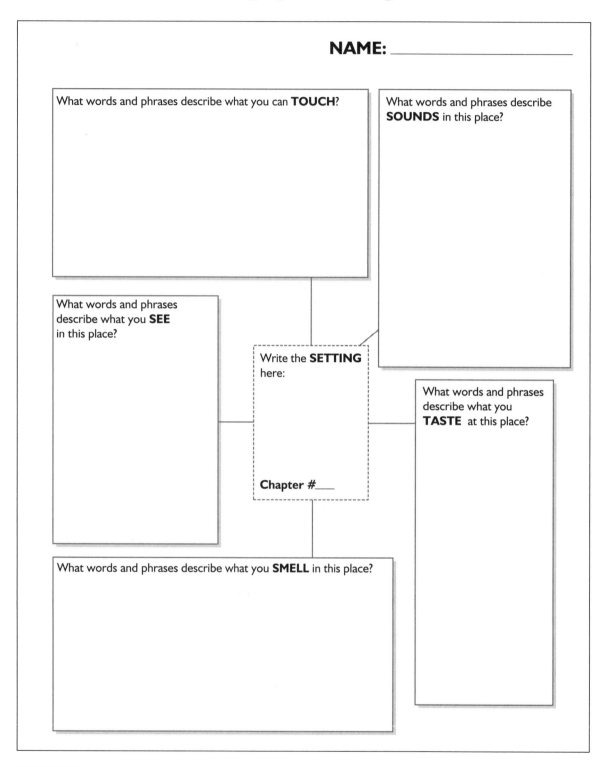

FIGURE 2.9

Setting Excerpt

On rocky islands gulls woke. Time to be about their business. Silently they floated in on the town, but when their icy eyes sighted the first dead fish, first bits of garbage about the ships and wharves, they began to scream and quarrel.

The cocks in Boston back yards had long before cried the coming of the day. Now the hens were also awake, scratching, clucking, laying eggs.

Cats in malt houses, granaries, ship holds, mansions and hovels caught a last mouse, settled down to wash their fur and sleep. Cats did not work by day.

In stables horses shook their halters and whinnied.

In barns cows lowed to be milked.

Boston slowly opened its eyes, stretched, and woke. The sun struck in horizontally from the east, flashing upon weathervanes—brass cocks and arrows, here a glass-eyed Indian, there a copper grasshopper—and the bells in the steeples cling-clanged, telling the people it was time to be up and about.

FIGURE 2.10

Source: Excerpt from *Johnny Tremain*, by Esther Forbes (1943), p. 1.

Descriptive Setting Checklist

Write about a historical setting using as much imagery as you can. Use this Checklist to guide you while writing.

Ideas/Content and Organization and Word Choice

- ☐ I write about a **historical setting that complements the novel** and **is accurate.**
- ☐ I have **one clear main idea** and **stay on topic.**
- ☐ I write at least **one paragraph**. I correctly **indent**.
- ☐ I begin my paragraph(s) with a **topic sentence**.
- ☐ I include **specific and interesting details** about this place.
- ☐ I include **imagery** by focusing my writing on the senses: taste, touch, smell, see, and hear.
- ☐ I write descriptive **adjectives** and **verbs.**
- ☐ My **ending is complete** and does not repeat the beginning.
- ☐ I include an **original title.**

Descriptive Setting

Voice

- ☐ I use the same **point of view** throughout my paper.
- ☐ I know why I am writing **(purpose)** and to whom I am writing **(audience).**

Sentence Fluency

- ☐ I write **complete sentences** so there are no fragments.
- ☐ I have **no run-on sentences.**
- ☐ My **sentences begin in different ways.**
- ☐ I use a **variety of sentence types.**

Conventions

- ☐ I **spell** all words correctly. I use the dictionary for words I don't know how to spell.
- ☐ I use correct **punctuation** throughout my paper.
- ☐ I **capitalize** appropriate letters.
- ☐ My sentences make sense and do not have **grammar** errors.
- ☐ My **writing is legible**. It looks like I took good care of my paper because it is **neat**, too.

NAME:_____

FIGURE 2.11

Revision Sheet: Descriptive Setting

Descriptors	Circle the right answer:	
The writing focuses on a *descriptive setting.* The paper does not get off topic.	Yes	No
There are *no grammar or conventions errors* and the paper and handwriting are neat.	Yes	No
Proper *indentation* is used for paragraphing.	Yes	No

Descriptors	Ideas/Organization
The (or each) paragraph includes a *topic sentence* about a place. The assignment might call for a historical setting.	Write the topic sentence(s):
The writer includes *specific and interesting details* about the setting.	Write two specific and interesting details included in the paper: 1. 2.
The writer uses *imagery.*	Write one example of imagery:
	Write a second example of imagery:

FIGURE 2.12 *(Continued)*

Descriptors	Word Choice
The writer uses *strong word choice*.	Write two descriptive adjectives the author uses:
	Write two descriptive nouns the author uses:

Descriptors	Sentence Fluency
Sentences begin in different ways.	Write two sentences that begin in different ways: 1.
	2.
Different types of sentences are used; some are long and some are short sentences.	Write a long sentence example:
	Write a short sentence example:
The writer includes a *satisfying conclusion* that does not repeat the beginning.	Write a sentence from the conclusion that is originally stated:

Writer: _____   Reviewer: _____

FIGURE 2.12

Setting Rubric

	Components	Points
Idea Development/Content AND Word Choice	**Follows Assignment:** completely follows assignment guidelines	• Assignment guidelines clearly followed = **5** • Assignment guidelines followed; minor detail missing = **4** • Assignment guidelines generally followed; two minor details missing = **3** • Unclear about guidelines; length not appropriate = **2** • Did not follow assignment guidelines = **1**
	Quality of Details: specific and interesting details; setting complements novel; historically accurate	• Sophisticated specific and interesting details consistently used; setting complements novel; historically accurate = **10** • Specific and interesting details consistently used; setting complements novel; historically accurate = **8** • Specific details, some interesting details; setting complements novel; historically accurate = **6** • Details are vague and might be listed; setting somewhat complements novel; generally historically accurate = **4** • Poorly written details; setting has little connection to novel; not entirely historically accurate = **2**
	Vocabulary/Imagery: descriptive adjectives and verbs; no repetition; thoughtful and accurate use of imagery	• Consistently precise/accurate words; no repetition; sophisticated use of imagery throughout paper = **10** • Most words carefully chosen/accurate; no repetition; some sophisticated use of imagery = **8** • Words sometimes carefully chosen/accurate; minor repetition; strong imagery = **6** • Weak word choice and/or little accuracy; repetition; some imagery = **4** • Haphazardly chosen words; repetition; little, if any, imagery = **2**
Organization	**Introduction:** creative topic sentence	Excellent = **5**; Good = **4**; Average = **3**; Weak = **2**; No topic sentence = **1**
	Body Paragraph Structure: topic sentence, significant details, ending	Body paragraph clearly structured; all parts included = **5** or **4**; Body paragraph missing one element = **3**; Body paragraph missing two elements = **2**; Body paragraph structure altogether incomplete = **1**
	Conclusion: complete ending; does not repeat topic sentence	Excellent = **5**; Good = **4**; Average = **3**; Weak = **2**; No conclusion = **1**
	Title: original title	Excellent = **5**; Good = **4**; Average = **3**; Weak = **2**; No title = **1**

FIGURE 2.13 *(Continued)*

	Components	Points
Conventions/Presentation	**Neatness:** neat paper; legible penmanship	Very clean and clear = **5**; Clean and clear = **4**; Some messiness = **3**; Messy = **2**; Unacceptably messy = **1**
	Grammar: sentences make sense grammatically	No errors = **5**; One error = **4**; Two to three errors = **3**; Four to six errors = **2**; More than seven errors = **1**
	Conventions: proper punctuation, capitalization, and spelling	No errors = **5**; One error = **4**; Two to three errors = **3**; Four to six errors = **2**; More than seven errors = **1**
Voice	**Point of View:** written in same point of view throughout paper	Writer maintains same point of view throughout paper = **5**; Writer might get off track once = **3**; Haphazard use of point of view = **1**
	Purpose/Audience: writer clear about audience and purpose	Writer entirely clear about audience/purpose = **5**; Writer might get off track once = **3**; Writer unclear about audience/purpose = **1**
Sentence Fluency	**Sentence Beginnings:** variety of sentence beginnings	• Thoughtful use of sentence beginning variety = **5** • Usually uses sentence beginning variety = **4** • Sometimes uses sentence beginning variety = **3** • Most sentences begin in the same way = **2** • All sentences begin in the same way by either the same word or the same type (e.g., all subjects) = **1**
	Sentence Variety: variety of sentence types	Thoughtful use of sentence variety = **5**; Usually uses sentence variety = **4**; Sometimes uses sentence variety = **3**; Little sentence variety = **2**; No sentence variety = **0**
	Run-ons and Complete Sentences: includes complete sentences and no run-ons	No run-ons; all complete sentences = **5**; One run-on or one fragment = **4**; Two run-ons or fragments = **3**; More than two run-ons or fragments = **2**; Unclear about sentence structure altogether = **0**

FIGURE 2.13

Setting Rubric Recording Sheet

Student: _____

Highest Possible Points: 85

Total Points Attained: ____

Converted Letter Grade: ____

	Components	Points/Comments
Idea Development Content AND Word Choice	**Follows Assignment:** completely follows assignment guidelines	____ out of 25 possible
	Quality of Details: specific and interesting details; setting complements novel; historically accurate	
	Vocabulary/Imagery: descriptive adjectives and verbs; no repetition; thoughtful and accurate use of imagery	
Organization	**Introduction:** creative topic sentence	____ out of 20 possible
	Body Paragraph Structure: topic sentence, significant details, ending	
	Conclusion: complete ending; does not repeat topic sentence	
	Title: original title	
Conventions/ Presentation	**Neatness:** neat paper and legible penmanship	____ out of 15 possible
	Grammar: sentences make sense grammatically	
	Conventions: proper punctuation, capitalization, and spelling	
Voice	**Point of View:** written in third person consistently throughout paper	____ out of 10 possible
	Purpose/Audience: writer clear about audience and purpose	
Sentence Fluency	**Sentence Beginnings:** includes a variety of sentence beginnings	____ out of 15 possible
	Sentence Variety: variety of sentence types	
	Run-ons and Complete Sentences: includes complete sentences and no run-ons	

FIGURE 2.14

The 4-6-8-10 Rule

Vicki Spandel (2001) in her book *Creating Writers Through 6-Trait Writing Assessment and Instruction* created a mathematical conversion for arriving at letter grades from number scores. She states about this conversion: "You are not *giving* the student *anything*. You are simply making up for the fact that measurement on a continuum is by nature slightly imprecise, so we have to adjust it to make it fit our grading system." Here is how it works:

First, figure out the basic percentage for a student's paper. For example, if the paper is worth 80 points and a student scores a 68, the basic percentage is 85%. Now, add the conversion as shown below. For the 85% paper, the conversion would be 91%.

Conversion:

- For scores over 90%, add 4 points to the total.

  Example: 92 original percent + 4 = 96% conversion

- For scores over 80%, add 6 points to the total.

  Example: 85 original percent + 6 = 91% conversion

- For scores over 70%, add 8 points to the total.

  Example: 73 original percent + 8 = 81% conversion

- For scores over 60%, add 10 points to the total.

  Example: 69 original percent + 10 = 79% conversion

Note: For scores right on the edge (60, 70, 80, 90), add one additional point. For example, if the percentage is 80%, then add 80 + 6 + 1 to arrive at 87%.

FIGURE 2.15

DIFFERENTIATED LESSON SAMPLE #3

GUIDING—or ESSENTIAL—QUESTION

How do organisms interact and depend on one another through food chains or food webs in an ecosystem?

LESSON OVERVIEW/UNIT CONTEXT

Students will understand how organisms are connected through food chains and food webs in ecosystems and the implications of removing one of the organisms. This activity assumes that students have already studied food chains and food webs in various ecosystems.

STANDARDS

Science Standard 6

Understands relationships among organisms and their physical environment

- *Benchmark 3:* Knows ways in which organisms interact and depend on one another through food chains and food webs in an ecosystem (e.g., producer/consumer, predator/prey, parasite/host, relationships that are mutually beneficial or competitive)

CONCEPTS

Ecosystem, organism, environment, food chain, food web

SKILLS/ACTIVITIES

- Brainstorm a list of ecosystems.
- Select and research one ecosystem; create food chain or food web.
- Determine the effects of the absence of organisms on an ecosystem.

DIFFERENTIATION STRATEGIES

- *Readiness:* Various resources at varying levels of difficulty; modify by partially completing graphic organizers; modify questions for presentation and criteria used for assessment.
- *Learning style:* Work individually or in partners; choose type of presentation (e.g., visual, written, oral, etc.).
- *Interest:* Choose an ecosystem of interest.

RESOURCES/MATERIALS

- "Let's Review" (Figure 2.16)
- Resources for researching various ecosystems (e.g., nature magazines, textbooks, encyclopedias, the Internet) at various levels of difficulty
- Various materials for presentations (will vary depending on the type of presentations students choose to develop)
- Graphic organizer for food web or food chain (for struggling learners, as needed)
- "How Do Organisms Interact and Depend on One Another Through Food Chains or Food Webs in an Ecosystem?" student checklist (Figure 2.17)

TIMING

Three or four class periods (based on 43- to 50-minute class periods)

LESSON DETAILS

1. *Brainstorm a list of ecosystems.*

   - Solicit volunteers to define the term *ecosystem*. Arrive at a class definition and write it on the board. This lesson follows others where students have studied the term and read about it previously.

   - In groups of three to five, instruct students to use the Roundtable strategy to list various ecosystems. Read "Let's Review" (Figure 2.16) so you are clear about how to conduct this strategy. Show these directions on an overhead, SMARTboard, or document camera. The blank spaces allow you to use this strategy again for another lesson. Write "ecosystem" in the space for number 4 so students know they are listing examples of ecosystems (e.g., ocean, prairie, jungle, desert, high tundra, deciduous forest, etc.).

   - Instruct students to write their names at the top of the group paper. As they enter line items on the sheet, tell them to put their initials in parentheses next to their entries. When you collect these papers, you will know what students entered to give you informal, cursory information about their current knowledge base. Allow students to "pass" after they have entered what they can on the group sheet. Some members may keep rotating the paper making entries, while others are finished after a few rounds. Teachers employ differentiation as they observe students completing this activity and the actual entries they make or do not make by passing.

   - Title a piece of butcher paper "Ecosystems." After groups have finished entering all they can on their group sheets, invite one group at a time to state one ecosystem. Enter each item on the butcher paper. Continue calling on each group until all groups have had a chance to contribute items on their lists. As a class, review the list and delete any entries that are not examples of ecosystems.

2. *Select and research one ecosystem; create food chain or food web.*

   - Pose the guiding question to students to set the objective for the lesson: *How do organisms interact and depend on one another through food chains or food webs in an ecosystem?*

   - Tell students they will research an ecosystem and create a food chain or food web showing the interrelationships of organisms within that ecosystem. Show and distribute Figure 2.17, which provides a checklist they use as a guide for working on their food webs or chains and projects. Focus first on the creation of the chain or web that is shown at the top half of the checklist. They are to choose one major producer, consumer, or decomposer in the ecosystem to focus on and organize their food chain or food web so that it shows how this organism is directly or indirectly connected to other organisms in the food chain or food web.

     ▸ *Differentiated by interest:* Allow students to choose an ecosystem they find interesting as the focus for their food chain or web. They can select one from the class-generated list of ecosystems.

     ▸ *Differentiated by learning style:* Allow students to work individually or in pairs.

     ▸ *Differentiated by readiness:* (1) Provide resources at varying levels of difficulty for students to use. This can include textbooks or textbook excerpts from different grades, Internet Web sites, magazines, articles, books, and so forth. (2) Give struggling students a blank food chain or web to use; fill in some key spaces on the graphic organizer, as needed.

3. *Create a project that shows the effect of an organism missing from an ecosystem.*

- Instruct students to imagine that the selected organism that is the focus of their food chains or webs has suddenly disappeared from the ecosystem. Return to the checklist in Figure 2.17. Focus students' attention to the bottom half concerning the project and review it. Zero in on the line item that reads: "I follow the criteria that my class created as a guide for completing my project." Tell students they will select and create a project of their choice, but first we all need to create and agree on the criteria. Lead a brainstorming session with the class to identify and list the criteria for each project so students are clear about expectations before beginning. You might even have students work in small groups to design criteria for each project and then share and evaluate with the class so the criteria have similar levels of rigor.

- After students have worked on their projects, have them present to the class their food chains or webs along with a visual, written, oral, or multimedia project they created that addresses the following questions. Debrief the entire exercise by making sure to focus ample attention on the last question, which is the lesson guiding question.

  - *How might the other organisms be affected by the removal of this organism from the ecosystem?*
  - *Do you think the food chain or food web can continue without this organism?*
  - *What do you predict will eventually happen to the ecosystem as a result of the removal of this organism?*
  - *Based on your answers to the above questions, how would you describe the relationships that exist among organisms in food chains and food webs?*
  - *How do organisms interact and depend on one another through food chains or food webs in an ecosystem?*

    - *Differentiated by learning style:* (1) Students choose their type of presentation (e.g., visual, written, oral, etc.). (2) Students may work individually or in pairs.

    - *Differentiated by readiness:* (1) For struggling students, modify the questions that are included in the presentation. Make sure, however, that all students respond to the overarching lesson guiding question: *How do organisms interact and depend on one another through food chains or food webs in an ecosystem?* (2) Review the criteria the class generates and modify specific line items, as needed, for struggling students.

Extensions

Invite students to extend and connect their learning by finding current events on the environment and the effects of loss of species to summarize and share with the class.

ASSESSMENTS

(This is a recap of assessments throughout the lesson to show formal and informal evidence of student performance.)

- Observation and brainstorm list during "Roundtable"
- Food chain or food web
- Project and presentation
- Summary of current events (extension)

Source: Adapted with permission of McREL from http://www.mcrel.org/compendium/activityDetail.asp?activityID=96.

Let's Review (Roundtable Strategy)

1. Take out one piece of paper per group.

2. Each group member is to have a pen or pencil.

3. Raise your hand if your birthday is closest to _____. You are first. The person on your left is second so that the paper moves clockwise.

4. Starting with the first person, write down one word or phrase that you learned during our study of _____.

5. Each group member continues to pass the paper clockwise entering one word or phrase about what was learned.

6. No duplications are allowed, so read all the previous entries before writing yours. You are entitled to pass when the paper comes to you.

7. Time limit: _____.

FIGURE 2.16

How Do Organisms Interact and Depend on One Another Through Food Chains or Food Webs in an Ecosystem?

Use these checklists as a guide while working on your food chain/web and project.

Food Chain or Food Web

☐ I research an ecosystem using at least two resources.

☐ I create a food chain or food web that shows the interrelationships of organisms within my ecosystem.

☐ My food chain or food web is detailed and complete. It shows my understanding of the ecosystem.

☐ I choose one major producer, consumer, or decomposer as a focus. I organize my food chain or food web to show how this organism is directly or indirectly connected to other organisms in the food chain or food web.

Project

☐ I create a project that I present to the class about what would happen if my organism suddenly disappeared from the ecosystem.

☐ I follow the criteria that my class created as a guide for completing my project.

☐ In my project, I include answers to these questions:

• How might the other organisms be affected by the removal of this organism from the ecosystem?

• Do you think the food chain or food web can continue without this organism?

• What do you predict will eventually happen to the ecosystem as a result of the removal of this organism?

• Based on your answers to the above questions, how would you describe the relationships that exist among organisms in food chains and food webs?

FIGURE 2.17

Source: Adapted with permission of McREL from http://www.mcrel.org/compendium/activityDetail.asp?activityID=122.

DIFFERENTIATED LESSON SAMPLE #4

GUIDING—or ESSENTIAL—QUESTION

How can I construct a logical argument to justify my reasoning and conclusions?

LESSON OVERVIEW/UNIT CONTEXT

Students will understand the fallacy of a pyramid scheme by constructing a diagram or using manipulatives to represent a pyramid scheme situation. Based on ideas from their representation, students construct an informal logical argument to explain the breakdown of the scheme.

STANDARDS

Math Standard I

Uses a variety of strategies in the problem-solving process

- *Benchmark 5:* Represents problem situations in and translates among oral, written, concrete, pictorial, and graphical forms.
- *Benchmark 7:* Construct informal logical arguments to justify reasoning processes and methods of solutions to problems (i.e., uses informal deductive methods).

CONCEPTS

Exponents, process

SKILLS/ACTIVITIES

- Create a diagram or use manipulatives.
- Construct logical argument.

DIFFERENTIATION STRATEGIES

- *Readiness:* Two versions of activity sheet to tier assignment.
- *Learning style:* Work individually or in pairs.

RESOURCES/MATERIALS

- *The King's Chessboard* by David Birch (Puffin Books)
- "How Can I Construct a Logical Argument to Justify My Reasoning and Conclusions?"— 2 versions: ♣♠ for at-grade-level students and high-achieving students; ♥ for struggling learners (Figures 2.18 and 2.19)

TIMING

Two or three class periods (based on 43- to 50-minute class periods)

LESSON DETAILS

1. *Read a picture book for conceptual introduction.*

   - Read the picture book *The King's Chessboard* by David Birch. This tale, which is set in ancient India, is a parable about a king and a wise man who poses a mathematical puzzle using a chessboard. The story is a vehicle to launch a discussion of exponential possibility so students can make a connection between this story and pyramid schemes, the focus for the lesson. The wise man uses the chessboard for a puzzle in which a single grain of rice is placed on the first square, two grains on the second square, four on the third square, and so on. The story not only focuses on math concepts but contains a social message as well.

2. *Explain pyramid schemes by providing an example.* Share the following scenario. As you do, model by showing how you would create a diagram or use manipulatives to demonstrate the situation.

   - Pyramid schemes depend on bringing in an exponentially growing number of new participants. If you start with one person, who gets 10 people to join, and each of those people get 10 more people to join, and so on, you have the total number of people growing by powers of 10.

   - The total number of people involved grows to amazingly huge numbers without very many steps being required to reach these huge numbers. But these huge numbers create a problem. (Ask, "Any idea what the problem might be?")

   - There are somewhere between 5 and 6 billion people in the world. Let's suppose that every one of these people could be induced to join a particular pyramid scheme. (Ask, "For how many levels could this scheme run before it failed for lack of new participants?")

   - You'll be amazed when you see how quickly the number of required new participants grows to exceed the population.

   - In this example, I assumed that each person who joined would bring in 10 new people. How many levels can be supported by a population of 5 to 6 billion? (Say, "Let's count them.")

   - That's 10 levels, counting the one person at the top who started it. By the time these 10 levels are filled, there will be a total of 1,111,111,111 participants. The 11th level would require 10,000,000,000 or 10 billion new participants to fill in.

   - But there aren't that many people in the world. There are only between 5 and 6 billion, minus the 1 billion plus who've already joined. Most of the billion people in the 10th level will not be able to get any new participants below them and will therefore make no money at all. And, of course, none of those who join in the 11th level will get any new participants below them. There aren't enough people to fill in the 11th level, much less to start a 12th level below that.

   - At this point, the pyramid collapses. And when it does, a solid majority of those who had joined will not have made any return at all. They will have paid their money to get in, but the promise that they will profit as people join below them will never be fulfilled.

3. *Present the assignment.*

   - Pose the guiding question to students to set the objective for the assignment: *How can I construct a logical argument to justify my reasoning and conclusions?* Refer to the diagram or manipulatives you used as you presented the scenario.

- Explain the assignment students will complete. Distribute one of the two assignment sheets based on student readiness.
  - ▶ *Differentiated by readiness:* Distribute the version with the club and spade (♣ ♠) in Figure 2.18 to at-grade-level and high-achieving students. Give the heart version (♥) in Figure 2.19 to struggling learners and provide adult assistance, as needed.
  - ▶ *Differentiated by learning style:* Allow students to work individually or in pairs.

Extensions

- Students can further their understanding about pyramid schemes through this or other Web sites: http://www.investopedia.com/articles/04/042104.asp. After reading, they can summarize the major points about pyramid schemes and present their findings to the class.
- Two companies—Amway and Mary Kay—offer products to consumers, such as household goods and cosmetics. They are therefore considered multilevel marketing businesses as opposed to pyramid schemes. Have students research one or both companies and explain to the class (or teacher) the similarities between multilevel marketing and pyramid schemes.

ASSESSMENTS

(This is a recap of assessments throughout the lesson to show formal and informal evidence of student performance.)

- Diagram or manipulative design with written argument
- Summary of pyramid scheme (extension)
- Explanation of the similarities between multilevel marketing and pyramid schemes (extension)

Source: Adapted with permission of McREL from http://www.mcrel.org/compendium/activityDetail.asp?activityID=122.

♣ How Can I Construct a Logical Argument to Justify My Reasoning and Conclusions? ♠

Situation:

Your friend Darcy just received a chain letter in the mail that guarantees to make her some easy cash. The letter contains a list of two people and directs her to send $100 to the name at the top of the list. She is then supposed to remove the person's name from the top of the list, put her name at the bottom of the list, and send it to 10 of her friends. The letter goes on to explain how she will end up receiving letters containing $100 from 100 people—netting her $10,000.

This sounds like a great plan to Darcy because all her friends will make money, and their friends, and their friends . . . but will it be fair to everyone? At some point, there will be no one left to sell it to because everyone else is on the list.

Assignment:

Use a diagram or manipulatives to represent the situation. Based on ideas from your representation, construct an informal logical argument to explain how the chain-letter scheme will break down before everyone in the world gets $10,000.

FIGURE 2.18

Source: Used with permission of McREL from http://www.mcrel.org/compendium/activityDetail.asp?activityID=122.

♥ How Can I Construct a Logical Argument to Justify My Reasoning and Conclusions? ♥

Situation:

Your friend Mary just received a chain letter in the mail that guarantees to make her some easy cash. The letter contains the name of one person and directs her to send $10 to her. She is then supposed to remove the person's name and send it to 5 of her friends. The letter goes on to explain how she will end up receiving letters containing $10 from 10 people—netting her $100.

This sounds like a great plan to Mary because all her friends will make money, and their friends, and their friends . . . but will it be fair to everyone? At some point, there will be no one left to sell it to because everyone else is on the list.

Assignment:

Use a diagram or manipulatives to represent the situation. Based on ideas from your representation, construct an informal logical argument to explain how the chain-letter scheme will break down before everyone in the world gets $100.

FIGURE 2.19

Source: Adapted with permission of McREL from http://www.mcrel.org/compendium/activityDetail.asp?activityID=122.

3

Standards, Concepts, and Guiding Questions

I am convinced of the following: If teachers take the time to critically view standards and cull concepts from them, and then write guiding (or essential) questions using these standards and concepts to serve as their guidepost for designing curriculum, students would have a more meaningful classroom experience. I realize that sounds like a tall order. But bear with me, and I promise that you will be enlightened, too. When I was in the classroom, my teaching improved dramatically as a result of using guiding questions. As I structured every activity, every assignment, every task, every lesson, every assessment within the framework of a guiding question, I not only held myself accountable to standards and concepts embedded within them, but I helped my students learn the core of the content. When working with teachers who utilize guiding questions, they, too, experience positive results. The premise for using these questions is to guide students to comprehend the essence of the content, know the concepts that drive each lesson, and maximize their learning potential by gleaning the heart of the curriculum instead of focusing on isolated skills or topics.

Differentiated instruction relies heavily on guiding questions, which other academicians also call essential questions. (The terms are interchangeable, but I will continue to use *guiding questions*.) They allow teachers to stay focused on the goals of a lesson and unit and create differentiated opportunities that stay true to these questions so all students are exposed to the core of learning. For example, a question for a math unit might be *"How do people calculate given percentages of quantities and solve problems involving discounts?"* A teacher can pose different math prompts to groups based on ability levels but keep the integrity of the standards-based question by having all students respond to the overarching concepts of percentages, problem solving, and discounts. The high-achieving students would have a math prompt that is more complex and involved than a group comprised of struggling students.

In this chapter, I will define guiding questions, illustrate how to use standards and concepts to create these questions, and provide a number of examples. Standards are necessary for creating guiding questions and pinpointing concepts, and teachers are held accountable to satisfying district and state mandates. The trio of questions, standards, and concepts are intertwined in creating sound curriculum.

Many educational experts have written about and support the use of guiding questions as a cornerstone of teaching. Lynn Erickson (2002) in *Concept-Based Curriculum and Instruction: Teaching Beyond the Facts* defines guiding questions as "a critical driver for teaching and learning. They engage students in the study and create a bridge between performance-based activities and deeper, conceptual understandings." Heidi Hayes Jacobs (1997) states: "The essential question is conceptual commitment. In a sense you are saying, 'This is our focus for learning. I will put my teaching skills into helping my students examine the key concept implicit in the essential question.'" Wiggins and McTighe (1998) write this about guiding questions in *Understanding by Design:* "[The purpose is] to frame the learning, engage the learner, link to more specific or more general questions, and guide the exploration and uncovering of important ideas." In short, using guiding questions is not a novel educational idea, but a sound one that has spanned several decades. Teachers of differentiated classrooms are prime candidates for using these questions so that the various activities they devise for different configurations of students have the same overarching focus. Some worry that the basic-level students are relegated to drill-and-kill methods, whereas the high achievers get the advantage of more sophisticated and intriguing curriculum. Creating and using guiding questions keeps teachers focused on the goals for *all* students so they can plan equally engaging curriculum to satisfy individual needs. In fact, the expectation of differentiated instruction is that all students have equally engaging work, even as they work on diverse tasks that are tied to the overarching goals.

What typically happens is that teachers find or receive lessons from a variety of sources, for example, by accessing Web sites, receiving lessons from colleagues, and finding them in educational journals and textbooks. Guiding questions are like the spine and the lessons and activities are like vertebrae. The guiding questions provide the framework necessary to make meaning and connections for students from each learning opportunity instead of presenting lessons, activities, and assessments in isolation. To illustrate this point, I will share an experience from a teacher I worked with on a curriculum mapping project. I asked her to tell me what she did in a particular unit of study, and she detailed a listing of sound and meaningful activities she conducts that emanate from standards. A partial list of activities follows:

- Show pictures of the negative effects of environmental abuse; compare with pristine environment; note differences and identify causes.

- Tour a local recycling plant; list the benefits of recycling.

- Collect recyclable materials in various classrooms at school.

- Visit a local beach or park and clean up the debris.

- Separate various discarded materials and determine which is garbage and which is recyclable.

- Discuss and write a response to the prompt: "What can you do to help the earth?"

After some discussion, she admitted that although she thought the activities were meaningful, there was something missing in the unit. It seemed fragmented to her, but she didn't know how to make the overall unit more effective. I then shared my experiences and the research about guiding questions. I suggested that she structure each task and assessment within a series of conceptually based guiding questions that serve as the basis for her unit. We brainstormed these guiding questions after perusing content standards and the goals she wanted to accomplish: *How do human actions modify and affect the environment? How can individuals share responsibility for protecting the environment? Why should individuals take responsibility for protecting the environment? How does recycling generate environmental, financial, and social benefits?* She then discovered the missing link and was committed to teaching the same unit using one or more of the guiding questions from the brainstormed list as the basis for curriculum and instruction so students could see the overarching concepts when they perform each assignment or assessment. Before she conducted each task, she introduced the associated guiding question so students could see the purpose of their work.

One significant way to improve your teaching and help maximize student learning is through a standards-based curriculum organized and delivered around meaningful guiding questions. Even the exercise of creating the questions helps clarify exactly what the standards mean and what to teach. To this end, guiding questions must be created at the beginning of the unit to serve as a crystallization and translation of the standards, a guide for lesson and unit development that includes differentiation, and a clear vision for students so they can see what the whole unit involves and how each lesson fits within the greater scope. What I have described is a version of backward design (Wiggins & McTighe, 1998, 2005) because teachers begin with the goals of the unit firmly in mind before they begin planning individual lessons.

In Figure 3.1, you will find unit and lesson guiding questions for a novel study that culminates in a personal narrative. To arrive at these questions, teachers scoured standards and thought critically about the essence of the unit. Notice that the *unit* guiding questions all begin with

Unit Guiding Questions (GQ) With Associated Lesson Guiding Questions

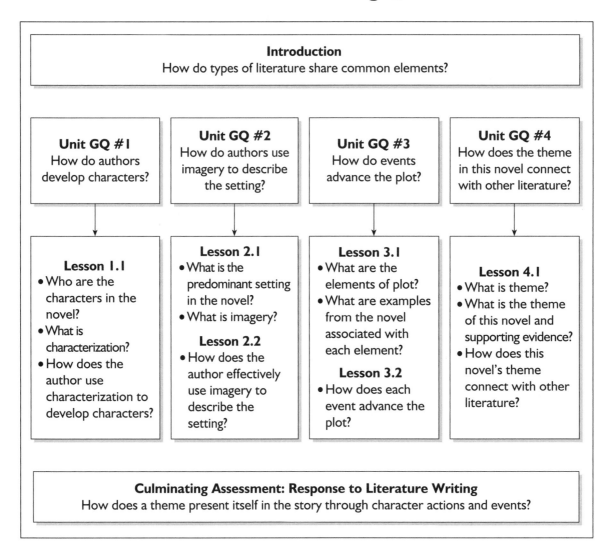

FIGURE 3.1

"why" or "how" so that they are more global and conceptual instead of detail oriented or skill focused. The *lesson* questions underneath can begin with any question word and are scaffolded in the order for teaching. Teachers start with a more rudimentary or introductory lesson question as the basis for arriving at the larger unit question, which accounts for the lessons sequenced the way they are—foundational questions leading to the overarching unit question. All questions should be written in language that is accessible to the level of students you are teaching. Naturally, questions designed for ninth-grade students include more sophisticated vocabulary than for fourth graders, but both will include targeted concepts.

As you read examples of guiding questions in this chapter, think about how they can be used in more than one lesson or unit in your curricular area and also other units in different grades and even across subjects. If applicable, I encourage teachers to use the same guiding questions in subsequent lessons and units and across grades if they apply because it helps students to see transference within a particular subject area and into other content areas. Since various concepts are included in the questions, it follows that they apply to related areas of study within one or more content areas. For example, in social studies a guiding question for a unit might be *"How does intolerance and fear lead to unspeakable actions?"* Teachers of various grade levels can use this question in a social studies class when teaching the Holocaust, the Salem witch trials, Native Americans, explorers, Japanese internment, and the Crusades. During language arts, teachers can use this same question when teaching certain novels such as *Maniac Magee, Witch of Blackbird Pond*, or *Roll of Thunder, Hear My Cry.* Students therefore elicit much more meaning when they see the connections. This quote aptly illustrates my point: "When we're teaching about the Holocaust, I think it's important for students to realize it's not something that happened once in our history, but that genocide is an issue that erupts around the world in situations of intense racial or ethnic conflict," said Gayle Y. Thieman (2007), president of the National Council for the Social Studies.

The same question (or similarly written questions that apply to particular grade levels) can be used across grades and addressed with more sophisticated lessons as students advance from grade to grade. For example, a fourth-grade question for the environment might be *"How do people's actions affect the environment in good and bad ways?"* In ninth grade, students address the unit question *"How do human actions modify and affect the environment?"*

In this chapter, you will find detailed step-by-step answers to these two guiding questions along with examples and tools to help you create guiding questions and implement them into your teaching: *How do teachers develop unit and lesson guiding questions? How do teachers use guiding questions in the classroom?*

HOW DO TEACHERS DEVELOP UNIT AND LESSON GUIDING QUESTIONS?

Identify Concepts Within Standards

Worthwhile lessons and units are centered on concepts and guided by standards, so guiding questions must incorporate both. The first step in crafting these questions is to identify the national, district, state, or school standards you intend to teach and find the concepts embedded within these targeted standards. A concept, as stated in Chapter 2, is a "one- or two-word mental construct that is broad and abstract, timeless, universal, and represents a variety of examples that all share the attributes of the concept" (Erickson, 2002). *Transportation, migration, symmetry,* and *conflict* are examples of concepts. Figure 3.2 features concepts that are subject specific and also macroconcepts that can apply to any subject area and are more overarching. Each list is not finite, so you might add other concepts to it. Teachers who design interdisciplinary units focus on macroconcepts to

Concepts

Science	Social Studies	Math
Adaptability	Change	Algebra
Change	Civilization	Data Analysis
Conservation	Conflict	Estimation
Diversity	Culture	Geometry
Energy	Democracy	Logical Reasoning
Environment	Diversity	Measurement
Evolution	Economy	Number
Genetics	Exploration	Order
Gravity	Geography/Climate	Pattern
Light	Government Systems	Proportions
Magnetism	Immigration/Migration	Ratio
Matter	Interdependence	Statistics/Probability
Organism	Justice	Symmetry
Scale and Structure	Politics	
Scientific Method	Religion	
Systems	Social Systems	
	Transportation	

Visual Arts	Language Arts	Health
Aesthetic	Cause/Effect	Body System
Balance	Change	Diet
Color	Conflict	Disease
Contrast	Exposition	Drugs
Form	Figurative Language	Exercise
Line	Foreshadowing	Family
Pattern	Literary Devices	Hygiene
Perspective	Metacognition	Illness
Shadow	Motivation	Nutrition
Shape	Narration	Puberty
Texture	Patterns	Wellness
Unity	Perspective/Point of View	
	Persuasion	
	Purpose	
	Stereotype	
	Structure	
	Symbolism	
	Theme	

FIGURE 3.2 (Continued)

Macroconcepts (broad, interdisciplinary concepts):		
Change	Interdependence	Pattern
Community	Movement	Perspective
Identity	Order	Structure
		System

FIGURE 3.2

integrate several subject areas. The following examples of standards have implied or stated concepts in italics:

- McREL Science Standard 9: Understands the sources and properties of *energy*

  Benchmark 8. Knows ways in which *light* interacts with *matter* (e.g., transmission, including refraction; absorption; scattering, including reflection)

- McREL U.S. History Standard 3: Understands why the Americas attracted Europeans [*immigration*], why they brought enslaved Africans [*slavery*] to their colonies, and how Europeans struggled for control of North America and the Caribbean [*conflict*]

  Benchmark 3. Understands peaceful and conflicting *interaction* between English settlers and Native Americans in the New England, Mid-Atlantic, Chesapeake, and lower South colonies (e.g., how Native American and European societies influenced one another [*society, culture*], differing European and Native American views of the land and its use [*perspective*])

Craft Unit Guiding Questions

Although this book focuses mainly on lesson design, it is critical that you are aware of the spectrum of the entire unit so that each lesson has context. For this reason, I am explaining how to craft both unit and lesson guiding questions. As discussed in reference to Figure 3.1, unit guiding questions are more all-encompassing than the lesson guiding questions, which are scaffolded and intended to get students to ultimately respond to the unit guiding question. The discussion here focuses on crafting unit guiding questions; see Figure 3.3 for brainstormed examples of standards-based unit questions. Subsequently, I will explain how to create lesson guiding questions since these should be designed and taught within a unit framework.

Standards are sometimes overwhelming and difficult to understand. It is challenging but wholly necessary for teachers to decipher standards in order to get at the essence of what should be taught. Unit guiding questions are the result of the arduous and meaningful task of critically

Sample Unit Guiding Questions

Possible Standards	Possible Unit Guiding Questions
Literature: Comprehension and Analysis	
Reading Standard 6: Uses reading skills and strategies to understand and interpret a variety of literary texts	
• *Benchmark 2:* Knows the defining characteristics of a variety of literary forms and genres (e.g., fiction, nonfiction, myths, poems, fantasies, biographies, autobiographies, science fiction, drama)	• How does the structure of a novel compare with other literary forms and genres?
• *Benchmark 3:* Understands complex elements of plot development (e.g., cause-and-effect relationships; use of subplots, parallel episodes, and climax; development of conflict and resolution)	• How is the plot influenced by setting? • How do authors develop a plot that includes compelling suspense? • How are conflicts addressed and resolved throughout the story?
• *Benchmark 4:* Understands elements of character development (e.g., character traits and motivations; stereotypes; relationships between character and plot development; development of characters through their words, speech patterns, thoughts, actions, narrator's description, and interaction with other characters; how motivations are revealed)	• How do authors develop characters through methods of characterization? • How do characters' actions, motivations, and beliefs affect the plot?
• *Benchmark 8:* Understands point of view in a literary text (e.g., first and third person, limited and omniscient, subjective and objective)	• How does a story's point of view influence readers' perceptions? • How does a change in point of view affect the original story?
• *Benchmark 9:* Understands inferred and recurring themes in literary works (e.g., bravery, loyalty, friendship, good v. evil; historical, cultural, and social themes)	• How do readers support the theme of this story with concrete evidence? • How is the theme similar across other literary works?
Contributions, Impact, and Achievements of Civilizations	
World History Standard 8: Understands how Aegean civilization emerged and how interrelations developed among peoples of the Eastern Mediterranean and Southwest Asia from 600 to 200 BCE • *Benchmark 2:* Understands the role of art, literature, and mythology in Greek society (e.g., major works of Greek drama and mythology and how they reveal ancient moral values and civic culture; how the arts and literature reflected cultural traditions in ancient Greece) (7th–8th grade)	• How did cultural achievements impact politics and the economy? • How did civilizations' achievements and contributions impact other societies then and now? • Why and how did laws in civilizations develop to govern society? • How did government evolve over time to meet societies' needs?

FIGURE 3.3 *(Continued)*

Possible Standards	Possible Unit Guiding Questions
• *Benchmark 5:* Understands the impact and achievements of the Hellenistic period (e.g., major lasting achievements of Hellenistic art, mathematics, science, philosophy, and political thought; the impact of Hellenism on Indian art) (7th–8th grade) • *Benchmark 1:* Understands the legacy of Greek thought and government (9th–12th grade)	• How did factors of a civilization hinder or encourage the arts? • How did philosophers influence and impact social order in civilizations? • How did leaders create change or continuity in societies?
World History Standard 9: Understand how major religious and large-scale empires arose in the Mediterranean Basin, China, and India from 500 BCE to 300 CE • *Benchmark 1:* Understands the significant individuals and achievements of Roman society (7th–8th grade) • *Benchmark 7:* Understands the political legacy of Roman society (9th–12th grade) • *Benchmark 2:* Understands influences on the economic and political framework of Roman society (7th–8th grade)	
Math	
Math Standard 2: Understands and applies basic and advanced properties of the concepts of *numbers* • *Benchmark 7:* Understands the concepts of ratio, proportion, and percent and the relationships among them	• How are ratio and percent related? • How does knowing the relationship between ratio, proportion, and percent help me solve problems?
Math Standard 4: Understands and applies basic and advanced properties of the concepts of *measurement* • *Benchmark 2:* Solves problems involving perimeter (circumference) and area of various shapes (e.g., parallelograms, triangles, circles)	• How are problems solved involving the area of various shapes? • How is the area of a given shape determined?
Math Standard 6: Understands and applies basic and advanced concepts of *statistics and data analysis* • *Benchmark 6:* Organizes and displays data using tables, graphs (e.g., line, circle, bar), frequency distributions, and plots (e.g., stem-and-leaf, box-and-whiskers, scatter) • *Benchmark 8:* Understands that the same set of data can be represented using a variety of tables, graphs, and symbols and that different modes of representation often convey different messages (e.g., variation in scale can alter a visual message)	• How can people organize, display, and analyze data? • How can data be represented in various ways to convey different messages? • How can the way in which a question is asked influence data results? • How can the ways in which results are displayed influence conclusions reached?

FIGURE 3.3 *(Continued)*

Possible Standards	Possible Unit Guiding Questions
The Behavior and Interaction of Light	
Science Standard 12: Understands the nature of scientific inquiry • *Benchmark 3:* Designs and conducts a scientific investigation (e.g., formulates hypotheses, designs and executes investigations, interprets data, synthesizes evidence into explanations, proposes alternative explanations for observations, critiques explanations and procedures) • *Benchmark 5:* Uses appropriate tools (including computer hardware and software) and techniques to gather, analyze, and interpret scientific data	• How do scientists conduct investigations using the scientific process? • How do scientists determine which tools and techniques to use to gather, analyze, and interpret scientific data?
Science Standard 9: Understands the sources and properties of energy • *Benchmark 4:* Knows how the sun acts as a major source of energy for changes on Earth's surface (i.e., the sun loses energy by emitting light; some of this light is transferred to Earth in a range of wavelengths including visible light, infrared radiation, and ultraviolet radiation) • *Benchmark 8:* Knows ways in which light interacts with matter (e.g., transmission, including refraction; absorption; scattering, including reflection) • *Benchmark 9:* Knows that only a narrow range of wavelengths of electromagnetic radiation can be seen by the human eye; differences of wavelength within that range of visible light are perceived as differences in color	• How does light behave and travel? • How does light interact with matter? • How is white light part of a greater energy spectrum? • How does the eye perceive light?

FIGURE 3.3

analyzing standards to pinpoint concepts and the relationship among them. For example, read these two questions: (1) *Why is setting important?* (2) *How does setting influence the plot?* In question #1, *setting* is the single concept. There is not another concept that begs for a relationship. So, what about setting? Nothing really other than it's important, which is nebulous. In question #2, *setting* and *plot* are both concepts. It's the verb *influence* that creates an association between these two concepts. For unit guiding questions, the goal is to try to craft the question so that there is a relationship between two concepts to make the question broader, more global, and less discrete. There certainly are times when it is difficult to write a question that includes a relationship between two concepts, but make sure to at least include a concept in the question. To create relationships, first identify the

Verbs That Show Relationships

account	develop	manipulate
account for	devise	map
advance	differentiate	modify
affect	discriminate	offer
alter	distinguish	organize
apply	employ	perceive
assess	evolve	point to
associate	examine	produce
build	expand	propose
cause	explain	relate
change	expound	separate
classify	express	sequence
compare	formulate	show
comprise	generate	simplify
construct	identify	solve
contrast	impact	structure
contribute	infer	transfer
convert	influence	transform
create	integrate	translate
demonstrate	interact	use
describe	interpret	utilize
design	lead to	uncover
determine	manage	

FIGURE 3.4

concepts and then ask yourself, "What about them?" It's the "what about them?" that helps formulate the relational component. In Figure 3.4, you will find a partial list of verbs that can be used to create this association.

Unit guiding questions should be written so that students are disinclined to answer with a list or perfunctory responses. In addition to writing questions with concepts and relationships, unit guiding questions will foster more meaningful inquiry if you begin each query with "why" or "how" as Lynn Erickson (2002) states in *Concept-Based Curriculum and Instruction*. Lesson guiding questions can begin with any question word and are taught in a specified order to ultimately arrive at the broader unit question.

Since standards are often quite cumbersome, it is important to note that you might meet facets of the same standards in different units. Keep this in mind when you address standards and write guiding questions. If you feel you do not satisfy the entire standard in a given unit, then determine where you will meet the missing points of the standard elsewhere in your curriculum.

To write your own **unit** guiding questions:

1. *Obtain your district, state, or school standards.* Locate the standards or benchmarks for the unit you will teach.

2. *Circle the concepts* embedded in each standard or benchmark. Or record any inferred concepts (e.g., standard states: *enslaved Africans;* concept: slavery). Use Figure 3.2, "Concepts," as a guide.

3. *Peruse the brainstormed lists of "Sample Unit Guiding Questions"* in Figure 3.3. Note that these unit guiding questions begin with "how" or "why." They also include concepts and sometimes relationships among them.

4. *Use the concepts you circled or recorded from your standards to brainstorm a comprehensive list of conceptually based questions.* Since you are brainstorming, write down all questions that come to mind even if they are slightly dissimilar. Later you can refine and edit the list. If it makes sense, create connections among the concepts when you craft your unit questions. As mentioned previously, avoid something like "How is the setting important?" and strive for "How does setting influence the plot?" Use Figure 3.4, "Verbs That Show Relationships," to assist you. Some like to create unit guiding questions void of a specific unit's topic so they are more universal, such as, "How does conflict affect people's lives politically, economically, and socially?" An alternative example is, "How did the American Revolution affect people's lives politically, economically, and socially?" The advantage to more global language is that it can be used across grade levels and units of study, but if you want to write them specific to your unit of study, you can easily make the transference for students. Another option is making the unit guiding question universal and creating lesson guiding questions geared to the unit of study. Example of unit guiding question: *How can government systems fail?* Examples of associated lesson guiding questions: *What were the main features of the Articles of Confederation? How did they fail to serve the people of the New World?*

5. *Write questions so students can understand them.* Since these questions navigate and focus students during the unit, make sure they are written in a language that they can understand. It is fair game to include words such as *irony* or *mitosis* or *culture* in a unit or lesson guiding question if teachers will be using these terms repeatedly during instruction and expect students to know and apply them. If there are words unfamiliar to students, make sure they are terms you plan to teach; otherwise, omit them. You do not want kids tripping over words to understand a guiding question, for example, *"How do readers extrapolate knowledge from multifarious sources?"* Rather, state the question using terms students know or will study in the unit: *"How do readers make inferences from various sources?"*

6. *Review your brainstormed list of unit guiding questions and narrow them down.* Make sure they are discrete so that there is no overlap. For example, you do not want two questions such as "How do people

affect the environment?" and "How do human actions influence the environment?" It is not unusual that you would have a brainstormed list with slightly similar questions, but choose the one among a similar list that is written in language most suitable to your students and that addresses the goals of the unit. After narrowing down a brainstormed list, here is a grouping of earth science standards and accompanying unit guiding questions:

Earth Science (ES) Standards:

ES 3—Water on Earth moves between the oceans and land through the processes of evaporation and condensation.

ES 4—Energy from the sun heats Earth unevenly, causing air movements that result in changing weather patterns.

ES 5—The solar system consists of planets and other bodies that orbit the sun in predictable paths.

Earth Sciences Unit Guiding Questions:

1. How does gravitational attraction keep objects in the solar system in orbit?

2. How does the process of evaporation and condensation redistribute water?

3. How is water recycled on Earth?

4. How do the sun and ocean affect weather?

5. How does energy from the sun heat Earth unevenly and cause a change in weather?

Source: Science Content Standards for California Public Schools Kindergarten Through Grade Twelve. California Department of Education, 2000. http://www.cde.ca.gov/be/st/ss/documents/sciencestnd.pdf

---

7. *Consider the number of questions.* Limit the number of unit guiding questions to no more than six, but use six only for longer units of study that are about six to eight weeks long. For shorter units, you may have only two or three unit questions. In terms of lesson guiding questions, there is no magic number of how many lessons you might conduct within each unit guiding question. Also, be cognizant of the time you have to teach and consider this as a factor. If you have only one to two weeks to teach an entire unit, then create one or two significant questions to accommodate your time constraints.

8. *Keep reading to learn how to design lesson guiding questions* that assist students to fully appreciate the goals of each unit. Remember to focus on the concepts, and phrase questions that apply to your students' developmental levels.

Craft Lesson Guiding Questions

Lesson guiding questions include at least one concept and represent a series of individual lessons you would conduct to help students answer each unit question. The lesson guiding questions will not necessarily show the conceptual relationship, but there should be a concept included in each one. For lesson guiding questions, I begin with any question word, unlike unit questions where I try to begin with "why" or "how" only. Teachers might want to include the unit guiding question as the last in the list of lesson guiding questions to remember that it is the overarching focus and must be addressed. The whole goal of the series of lesson guiding questions is to get students to understand and fully address the unit question. That means that some lesson guiding questions might focus more on getting students to perform discrete skills or respond to seemingly rudimentary questions. See the following example.

Unit Guiding Question	Lesson Guiding Questions
2. How does research writing influence or impact people's lives?	• Lesson 2.1: What are the types of research writing? • Lesson 2.2: Who are people who write research pieces? Why do they write this research? Who are their audiences? • Lesson 2.3: How does research writing influence or impact people's lives?

To write your own **lesson** guiding questions:

1. *Review Figure 3.1 again* to see an example of a novel study unit and lesson guiding questions plus the many examples in Figure 3.5: "Sample Unit and Lesson Guiding Questions."

2. *Follow the steps for creating unit guiding questions* previously delineated by reviewing standards, identifying concepts, brainstorming a list of possible questions, and narrowing the list so each lesson question is discrete. You will brainstorm a list of potential questions geared to each unit guiding question. It is not unusual to find in this brainstorming process that you want to tweak a unit guiding question. Like unit guiding questions, make sure the wording of your lesson guiding questions is not too sophisticated or confusing for your students.

3. *Sequence the questions.* Unit questions need to be sequenced as well as the individual lesson guiding questions within them. Once you have a list of unit questions, put them with the corresponding lesson guiding questions in an order that makes sense for teaching. Consider what unit guiding question would be appropriate for beginning the unit and which would be a suitable closing. Often, the first question can be the basis for an introductory lesson or series of lessons, and the last would represent the focus for a culminating activity as shown in Figure 3.1. But this is not always the case. The question for a novel unit—*"How do characters change throughout time?"*—is suitable for ongoing inquiry as students read the novel. It is also a question that can serve as the basis for a culminating response to a literature writing assignment in which students

Sample Unit and Lesson Guiding Questions

Standards	Unit Guiding Questions	Lesson Guiding Questions
Research Writing		
Reading Standard 7: Uses reading skills and strategies to understand and interpret a variety of informational texts. • *Benchmark 2:* Knows the defining characteristics of a variety of informational texts.	1. How does research writing compare to other forms of informational text?	• *Lesson 1.1:* What are different types of informational text? What are the purposes and audiences for each type? • *Lesson 1.2:* How is a research paper organizationally structured? How is the structure of a research paper different from other information text formats?
Reading Standard 7: Uses reading skills and strategies to understand and interpret a variety of informational texts. • *Benchmark 4:* Uses new information to adjust and extend personal knowledge base.	2. How does research writing influence or impact people's lives?	• *Lesson 2.1:* Why do people read research text? • *Lesson 2.2:* How can you or others benefit from reading and writing research papers or reports?
Writing Standard 1: Uses the general skills and strategies of the writing process. • *Benchmark 6:* Writes expository compositions (e.g., states a thesis or purpose; presents information that reflects knowledge about the topic of the report; organizes and presents information in a logical manner, including an introduction and conclusion; uses own words to develop ideas; uses common expository structures and features).	3. How do writers craft an informative, accurate, and organized research paper?	• *Lesson 3.1:* How do I write an informative introduction that includes a "hook" and thesis statement? • *Lesson 3.2:* How do I write topic sentences that link to the thesis? • *Lesson 3.3:* How do I use resources to find evidence that supports my thesis and topic sentences? How do I accurately cite these resources in a bibliography? • *Lesson 3.4:* How do I write evidence with important ideas, concepts, direct quotes, and paraphrasing? How do I accurately paraphrase information and write it in my own words? • *Lesson 3.5:* How do I write a satisfying conclusion?
Reading Standard 7: Uses reading skills and strategies to understand and interpret a variety of informational texts.	4. How do writers determine the reliability	• Lesson 4.1: How do I verify that my sources are legitimate and accurate?

FIGURE 3.5 (Continued)

Standards	Unit Guiding Questions	Lesson Guiding Questions
Benchmark 6: Differentiates between fact and opinion in informational texts.	and accuracy of informational resources and research?	• *Lesson 4.2:* What is the difference between subjective and objective sources?
Writing Standard 3: Uses grammatical and mechanical conventions in written compositions. • *Benchmark 8:* Uses conventions of spelling in written compositions. • *Benchmark 9:* Uses conventions of capitalization in written compositions. • *Benchmark 10:* Uses conventions of punctuation in written compositions. • *Benchmark 11:* Uses appropriate format in written compositions. **Writing Standard 2:** Uses the stylistic and rhetorical aspects of writing. • *Benchmark 2:* Uses paragraph form. • *Benchmark 3:* Uses a variety of sentence structures to expand and embed ideas. • *Benchmark 4:* Uses explicit transitional devices.	5. How do writers effectively edit and revise their work?	• *Lesson 5.2:* How do I edit my work for proper use of conventions and grammar? • *Lesson 5.1:* How can I use transitional words and phrases for more effective writing? • *Lesson 5.3:* How do I revise my paper to ensure proper organization, coherence, and sufficient evidence?
Government Systems		
United States History Standard 7: Understands the impact of the American Revolution on politics, economy, and society. • *Benchmark 3:* Understands the social, political, and economic effects of the American revolutionary victory on different groups.	1. How does conflict affect people's lives politically, economically, and socially?	• *Lesson 1.1:* What was the social and economical impact on individuals and families during the time of the American Revolution? • *Lesson 1.2:* What were the political effects of the American Revolution?

FIGURE 3.5 *(Continued)*

Standards	Unit Guiding Questions	Lesson Guiding Questions
United States History Standard 8: Understands the institutions and practices of government created during the Revolution and how these elements were revised between 1787 and 1815 to create the foundation of the American political system based on the U.S. Constitution and the Bill of Rights.	2. How can government systems fail?	• *Lesson 2.1:* What were the main features of the Articles of Confederation? • *Lesson 2.2:* How did they fail to serve the people in the New World?
United States History Standard 8: Understands the institutions and practices of government created during the Revolution and how these elements were revised between 1787 and 1815 to create the foundation of the American political system based on the U.S. Constitution and the Bill of Rights. • *Benchmark 3:* Understands the significance of the Bill of Rights and its specific guarantees (e.g., the relevance of the Bill of Rights in today's society) (5th–6th grade). • *Benchmark 2:* Understands arguments over the necessity of a Bill of Rights and Madison's role in securing its adoption by the First Congress (7th–8th grade). • *Benchmark 1:* Understands influences on the ideas established by the Constitution (9th–12th grade).	3. How do government systems balance group and individuals' rights?	• *Lesson 3.1:* How do the basic principles of democracy serve the people? • *Lesson 3.2:* What are the powers of each of the three branches of government? • *Lesson 3.3:* What major debates shaped the terms of the U.S. Constitution? How does the Constitution help protect citizens' rights by both empowering and limiting the federal government? • *Lesson 3.4:* What is the Bill of Rights, and why was it added to the Constitution? • *Lesson 3.5:* Why is it important for citizens to preserve the Constitution?
The Sun's Energy		
Standard 1: Understands atmospheric processes and the water cycle. • *Benchmark 3:* Knows that the sun is the principle energy source for phenomena on the Earth's surface (e.g., winds, ocean currents, the water cycle, plant growth).	1. How is the sun a source of energy?	• *Lesson 1.1:* How does the sun produce heat? • *Lesson 1.2:* How does the sun produce light?
	2. How does the sun's release of energy create different phenomena on Earth?	• *Lesson 2.1:* Where is the water found on Earth? • *Lesson 2.2:* How does water change phases?

FIGURE 3.5 *(Continued)*

Standards	Unit Guiding Questions	Lesson Guiding Questions
Standard 1: Understands atmospheric processes and the water cycle. • *Benchmark 7:* Knows that most of Earth's surface is covered by water, that most of that water is saltwater in oceans, and that fresh water is found in rivers, lakes, underground sources, and glaciers. • *Benchmark 2:* Knows the processes involved in the water cycle (e.g., evaporation, condensation, precipitation, surface run-off, percolation) and their effects on climatic patterns.	2. How does the sun's release of energy create different phenomena on Earth?	• *Lesson 2.3:* What are the processes of the water cycle? • *Lesson 2.4:* What are some of the variables that cause uneven heating of Earth's surface? • *Lesson 2.5:* How are convection currents produced? • *Lesson 2.6:* How does uneven heating of Earth's surface result in convection currents?
	3. How do plants use the sun's energy to produce their own food?	• *Lesson 3.1:* What is photosynthesis and how does it work? Why is photosynthesis important?
Coordinate Plane		
Standard 2: Understands and applies basic and advanced properties of the concepts of numbers. • *Benchmark 7:* Uses models (i.e., number lines) to identify, order, and compare numbers. • *Benchmark 1:* Understands the relationships among equivalent number representations (e.g., whole numbers, positive and negative integers) and the advantages and disadvantages of each type of representation. • *Benchmark 2:* Understands the characteristics and properties of the set of rational numbers and its subsets (e.g., whole numbers, fractions, decimals, integers). • *Benchmark 3:* Understands the role of positive and negative integers in the number system.	1. How do people add and subtract integers to solve real-life problems?	• *Lesson 1.1:* How can integers be represented on a number line? • *Lesson 1.2:* Why is it useful to add and subtract integers to solve real-life problems? • *Lesson 1.3:* How do I add and subtract integers to solve real-life problems?

FIGURE 3.5 *(Continued)*

Standards	Unit Guiding Questions	Lesson Guiding Questions
Standard 8: Understands and applies basic and advanced properties of functions and algebra. • *Benchmark 7:* Understands special values (e.g., minimum and maximum values, *x*- and *y*-intercepts, or slope) of patterns, relationships, and functions. • *Benchmark 9:* Uses the rectangular coordinate system to model and to solve problems.	2. How do people use the coordinate plane to solve real-life problems?	• *Lesson 2.1:* What are integer coordinates? • *Lesson 2.2:* How do I plot coordinates and evaluate the results? • *Lesson 2.3:* How do I use the coordinate plane to solve real-life problems?

FIGURE 3.5

examine the various ways characters change and evidence for the changes. Or the unit question *"How can leaders create change or continuity in societies?"* might be one teachers visit repeatedly in a Civil War or American Revolutionary War unit where there are leaders on both sides of the conflicts.

4. *Consider the number of questions.* Like unit guiding questions, you have to know your time limitations for teaching a unit. In terms of lesson guiding questions, there is no magic number of how many lessons you might conduct within each unit guiding question. However, I typically write no more than five lesson guiding questions per unit question. If there are more than five, the unit probably warrants an additional unit guiding question. I am also aware of my time frame for teaching each unit and plan my number of questions accordingly.

HOW DO TEACHERS USE GUIDING QUESTIONS IN THE CLASSROOM?

Focus Lessons, Activities, and Assessments Around Guiding Questions

Guiding questions are the impetus for teaching and learning, so make sure that each lesson you conduct, each activity you have students complete, and each assessment you devise all answer a unit or lesson guiding question. Essentially, everything you do in the classroom must answer a guiding question so you connect learning opportunities to something greater. Recall the metaphor of the guiding questions as the spine and the lessons and activities as the vertebrae. Without the spine to serve as a foundation, the vertebrae are unhinged and disconnected. If there is some time-honored activity or assessment that you have used year after year and it is successful in terms of meetings standards and unit goals, then there should be a guiding question for it. Create one if you haven't done so during planning. On the flip side, if you feel that the guiding questions you already have are enough, then reevaluate whether or not the activity or assessment is effective and meets curriculum goals. If not, then give yourself permission to nix it.

Remember that in a differentiated classroom, the guiding questions are the same for all students, but the lesson or activity or assessment in response to these questions can be differentiated. Use the questions as a guide and modify or extend learning to meet students' needs. You might also choose to devise an additional guiding question geared to the high-achieving student as an extension opportunity.

Display the Unit Guiding Questions

Make sure a list of the unit guiding questions is clearly visible to all students throughout the course of the unit. To do so, here are some options:

- Write the unit questions on a poster board or easel pad.
- Type them up and enlarge them at a copy shop. Then display them on a bulletin board or affix magnets or Velcro on the back of a piece of tagboard and post the questions on the whiteboard.

Sometimes teachers post the guiding questions at the beginning of the unit and share them with students immediately. Other times, you might begin the unit by investing students in the task of creating questions, and then post them. For example, you might ask students to brainstorm questions they might want to have answered within the unit. To take this approach, you could say: "We're beginning a unit on religions of the world. What questions would you want to investigate under this topic?" Then, evaluate their questions and use relevant ones as either unit or lesson guiding questions. In another scenario, teachers might first conduct a lab experiment, demonstration, or simulation that captures the interest of students. Afterwards, teachers can introduce and then post the unit guiding questions and connect the lab, demo, or activity to one particular guiding question. Displaying all unit guiding questions helps to remind students of the overarching goals and also provides context and connections for lessons, activities, and assessments so students have a clear focus for each task they undertake.

Use Unit and Lesson Guiding Questions to Set Objectives

Setting clearly defined objectives and sharing them with students is critical to effective teaching. Use both the unit and particular lesson guiding questions as a way to set objectives. As stated previously, post the unit questions at the outset of the unit for students to have a framework, or early on in the unit if a simulation is used to entice and stimulate learning. You can then use the lesson guiding questions to state objectives by communicating a particular lesson focus in question format. I am advocating the following approach to begin a lesson: "We have been studying about a period known as the Renaissance and its effect on European civilization. Today and tomorrow we will focus on the unit guiding question: *'How did the achievements of the Renaissance impact others?'* [Point to the unit question that is displayed.] We'll begin to tackle this unit question by answering: *'What were the achievements of the Renaissance?'* [Point to the lesson question that you have written under the day's agenda.]" When you structure objectives in question format, it helps students begin thinking about answers almost intuitively and gets their brains churning. Plus, introduce these questions in a compelling way to rouse interest. For instance, you might pose each question and share a brief story, show a picture that is eye-catching, or conduct a simulation to foster connections and intrigue.

SUMMARY

Standards, concepts, and guiding questions are a dynamic trio that teachers should use together to develop meaningful and effective curriculum. Those who have been charged with the responsibility of teaching kids use standards as a guide to formulate a curriculum that is spearheaded by conceptually based unit and lesson questions. Teachers hold themselves accountable to creating and conducting differentiated lessons, activities, and assessments in response to the questions. When students can respond coherently and accurately to a unit's essential questions and demonstrate what they learned, then a teacher should feel confident that the goals of a unit are met.

4

Assessment in a Differentiated Classroom

TYPES OF ASSESSMENTS

All types of assessments are critical for a sound, well-rounded unit of study, and they play a key role in a differentiated classroom. Therefore, I focus this chapter on defining the forms of assessments and providing various examples. Effective teachers administer and use a variety of assessments for different purposes and use this information to make learning beneficial for students. Preassessments are issued before a unit and sometimes even before a lesson to help teachers answer these questions: *What might students want to know or already know about a particular course of study? How do students learn best? What are their particular interests in a targeted area?* Formative—or ongoing—assessments are conducted throughout a unit and are woven into all lessons as teachers consider these questions: *How well do students understand a skill or concept I am currently teaching? What can they show me as proof of this understanding? How can I learn from students' responses and adjust my teaching appropriately?* At the end of a comprehensive unit of study, teachers assign summative assessments. These culminating products help teachers answer these questions: *How well did students grasp the concepts and understandings of this body of knowledge? How do the scores for a summative assessment indicate how well students have met standards?* In short, teachers frequently use a variety of assessments in a differentiated classroom to gather information so they can maximize students' learning and growth.

ASSESSMENT EXAMPLES

Because this book focuses on lesson planning, I devote much of this chapter to providing preassessment examples and also several differentiated formative assessments that serve to check for understanding and indicate further differentiation opportunities. The preassessments might be appropriate for some lessons, but typically preassessments are issued at the beginning of a series of lessons that represent a chunk of material or an entire unit. They can also double as formative assessments to check for understanding, so flag examples that resonate with you for both pre- and ongoing assessments with sticky notes.

I also include some assessments that can be used as either formative or summative depending on how you modify or extend these examples to meet lesson or unit goals. Remember that summative assessments are more substantial and suited for a unit culmination. Lastly, I share examples of summative assessments that are expressly for use at the end of a unit of instruction. A word to the wise: Be careful not to dismiss any example too quickly because it does not jive with the content area you teach. Instead, review it and see how you might adapt it for your purposes. It just might work!

Preassessments

Conducting a preassessment is prudent because it yields significant information about your students prior to beginning a lesson or unit. A well-written and well-administered preassessment gives you a clear understanding of students' current knowledge base, interests, or learning styles. You can use the results of a preassessment to plan instruction for an upcoming teaching opportunity to maximize student learning and differentiate instruction for individuals, groups of students, or the whole class. Preassessments allow you to determine whether or not students know skills before teaching a lesson and can also ascertain the conceptual level of student understanding. If the results of a preassessment show that three students are well versed in a particular concept or skill, it would not behoove these students to work in a whole-class setting and relearn what they already have shown they know. Instead, perhaps these students would benefit from a learning contract that allows them to work at a faster pace and explore a particular concept more fully. If you conduct a preassessment and learn that most of the class has mastered a particular skill, then the curriculum needs appropriate revision. That might mean instead of teaching a whole-class lesson, pull a few students who haven't yet become proficient in the skill and teach them privately. Other students can work on an anchor activity while you work alone with these other kids. An anchor activity could be reading a book, completing a written response, or working on another task that occupies students in a meaningful way.

The way preassessments are designed is important so that the results thoughtfully guide you in formulating and delivering differentiated curriculum. In readiness-based preassessments, teachers call on students to answer factual and conceptual information through formal methods (e.g., taking an objective test, solving math word problems, responding to short essays, drawing and labeling maps, creating webs to connect ideas, etc.) or informally (e.g., conversations with students, lab demonstration, using manipulatives, etc.) or both. Make sure to communicate to students that the preassessment will not be graded, but rather it is used to collect data about what students already know or are interested in so the lesson or unit meets their needs. Do not assume that because students have seemingly not been exposed to a topic, such as atomic theory or the American Revolution, that you cannot obtain information from a preassessment. You can ask questions to gather useful information about students' conceptual thinking. Knowing which students think at a higher level and to what extent can help you design learning activities to meet their particular needs, so do not disregard that goal when devising and issuing preassessments. Furthermore, some students may not have been previously exposed to specific curriculum, but they may learn the material at a faster pace. A preassessment can indicate which students can grasp concepts and skills faster than other students. For a preassessment to uncover this information about students, pay attention to how quickly they respond correctly on a repeated basis to written and oral tasks. To develop readiness-based preassessments, use existing unit resources and materials, textbook chapter quizzes and tests, and professional experts. In addition, teachers sometimes use these readiness-based preassessments as postassessments.

To glean information about what interests students and how they prefer to work, you may ask questions about subtopics within a unit of study that pique students' interests, types of projects they like to complete, proclivities to group configurations such as working independently as opposed to group work, and so forth. Books and Internet sites include several interest-based and learning-style surveys that you can use as samples for formulating such preassessments.

Following are several figures that show preassessment examples for you to use or adapt. They can function as a formative assessment, as well, to check for understanding. Among the preassessment examples, all except Figure 4.8 are preassessments designed to determine readiness level of students. This figure demonstrates an active participation strategy that you can employ to quickly and informally assess students. Here is an explanation of how you can use each preassessment featured in the figures:

Figure 4.1: Make a Web Preassessment

This preassessment is a precursor to a lesson or unit on a particular novel or short story. Students are expected to devise a web (or another graphic organizer) to show their understanding of the relationships of the terms listed, specifically, the elements of literature. In addition, students write a paragraph explaining their webs to articulate their thinking. I purposely do not title the preassessment because I want to know if students can determine which term fits in the center of the web. I walk around the room after I distribute this to see who might be struggling. For those

Make a Web Preassessment

1. On a separate sheet of paper, create a web using the following words and phrases in a way that you think makes sense. If you want to add your own words/phrases to your web, please do.

third person	plot	central conflict
when	character	introduction
first person	rising action	time
where	theme	place
point of view	falling action	elements
central message	antagonist	climax
setting	resolution	protagonist

2. Write a paragraph that explains your web.

FIGURE 4.1

completely stuck, I tell them "elements" is the web center so they can get started. I take mental notes of those who need support to begin or need little help to complete it. If you teach a subject other than language arts, certainly use this strategy by merely entering other terms associated with a unit of study for a discipline area you teach. Be sure to include a term for the web's center somewhere in your list of words and phrases.

Figure 4.2: Categorization Preassessment

This preassessment is quite straightforward. It allows teachers to determine who can categorize and define terms and apply their knowledge to the real world. The strategy can be easily adapted to other content areas or topics within science since it calls on students to categorize, define, and apply.

Figure 4.3: Terms Preassessment

Some students might have already mastered and use terms (or concepts or vocabulary) planned for a given course of study. If so, then they need the opportunity to show what they know so they can experience and learn new terms. This preassessment is a fairly simplistic readiness-based differentiation strategy that allows teachers to glean a great deal about what students already know prior to a lesson or unit of study. If they show clear understanding in

Categorization Preassessment

Directions: Use a separate sheet of paper to respond to the following. You will not be graded on this preassessment. I will use the information to help me plan this upcoming unit.

1. Make a T-chart. Title one column of the chart "renewable resources" and the other column "nonrenewable resources." Enter the words and phrases in the table below into whatever column makes sense to you.

fish	soil	biomass
tides	leather	reindeer
winds	solar power	coffee
oxygen	wind power	solar radiation
water	paper	coal
forests	gasoline	diesel
hydropower	natural gas	
wood	timber	

2. Define renewable resources.

3. Define nonrenewable resources.

4. How do you personally use a renewable *and* a nonrenewable resource? List the renewable and nonrenewable resource and be specific about how you use each. They do not have to be listed in the table above.

FIGURE 4.2

the preassessment for certain terms or concepts, you can provide alternative tasks so they are aptly challenged instead of asking them to repeat what they have proven they know. I wrote this preassessment for a math classroom, but teachers of other content areas can certainly adapt it for their purposes. In social studies, you can provide a list of concepts such as *revolution, immigration,* or *culture.* In language arts, students can replace familiar terms or vocabulary with others from a prepared list you provide to increase their word bank. In foreign language, the same principle applies.

Figure 4.4: Fact and Concept Preassessment

This preassessment provides an opportunity for students to show what facts and concepts they know. Even though some line items on the preassessment include content that students have not previously been exposed to, teachers can gather information about conceptual understanding.

Terms Preassessment

Directions: The following terms are the focus for our next math unit. Define any terms you know and provide an example as shown in the first line. Leave any lines blank if you wish. This is not graded; I will use it to help me plan instruction.

Math Terms	Definitions	Examples
Place value	The position of a digit in a number	The 2 in the number 200,000 is in the hundred thousands place.
Standard form		
Expanded form		
Whole number		
Decimal		
Equivalent decimals		
Round		
Estimate		
Variable		
Algebraic expression		
Evaluate		
Commutative Property		
Addend		
Identity Property		
Associative Property		

FIGURE 4.3

For example, students are asked to explain "all men are created equal" and "revolution." Teachers would benefit from knowing students' explanations even if they are not accurate in terms of the historical context. Higher-level thinking can emerge when responding to such questions. This would work in other content areas as well. For instance, in science, students can explain the water cycle or give examples of natural resources.

Figure 4.5: Rank Order

Students rank order world religions and estimate the number and percentages of adherents from provided lists. This assessment also allows teachers to see how well students can associate numbers to percentages. For math teachers, omit the ranking of specific religions and have students match percentages and associated numbers. Answers to Figure 4.5, which I got from the Web site http://www.adherents.com (2005), are as follows:

1. Christianity: 2.1 billion (33%)

2. Islam: 1.5 billion (21%)

3. Secular/Nonreligious/Agnostic/ Atheist: 1.1 billion (16%)

4. Hinduism: 900 million (14%)

5. Buddhism: 376 million (6%)

6. Sikhism: 23 million (0.36%)

7. Judaism: 14 million (0.22%)

This assessment can be adapted for other subject areas; for example, history teachers can provide a list of world events and ask students to rank

Fact and Concept Preassessment

AMERICAN INDEPENDENCE

Directions: You will not be graded on this assessment. It is for me to use to plan our upcoming unit based on what you already know or do not know. You may skip questions you do not have answers for, but you can also guess at an answer.

1. Number the following events in the order each happened by writing 1 for the first event, 2 for the second event, and so on in the spaces provided.

    _____ The Constitution was ratified (approved).
    _____ The War for American Independence (American Revolution) ends.
    _____ The Declaration of Independence is written.
    _____ The Boston Tea Party takes place.
    _____ George Washington presents his Farewell Address.

2. Explain what "all men are created equal" meant to most American leaders at the time the Declaration of Independence was written.

3. What does the word "revolution" mean?

4. How is the word "revolution" associated with early America and the colonists?

5. Tell briefly why each of the following persons, terms, or events is important. Use a separate sheet of paper for this.

a. Benjamin Franklin	e. George Washington	i. Articles of Confederation
b. Boston Massacre	f. Boston Tea Party	j. Declaration of Independence
c. Thomas Paine	g. Sons of Liberty	k. Loyalists
d. King George	h. Tories	l. Lexington and Concord

6. Using the blank map provided, write in the name of each colony that you know.

FIGURE 4.4

Rank Order

Directions: To complete this blank table about world religions, follow the directions below the table about what to write in each column. On the back, write down what you know about each religion, such as religious beliefs and practices, where the religion originated and is practiced today, and so on.

Religion (rank order)	Number of Adherents	Percentage of World Population

"Religion" Column: Below is a list of religions in random order. Rank order the religions according to the most number of adherents to the least number of adherents. Write the religions in your rank order in the table.

• Hinduism	• Buddhism	• Nonreligious (includes Agnostic and Atheist)
• Islam	• Christianity	
• Sikhism	• Judaism	

"Number of Adherents" Column: Below is a list of numbers in random order. Write a number next to each religion you ranked that shows the number of people who practice (or adhere to) this religion.

• 1.5 billion	• 1.1 billion	• 376 million
• 900 million	• 14 million	• 23 million
• 2.1 billion		

"Percentage of World Population" Column: Below is a list of percentage figures. Using the number of adherents you listed, write a percentage figure for each religious group.

• 0.36%	• 33%	• 21%
• 0.22%	• 6%	• 14%
• 16%		

FIGURE 4.5

order them from most to least important in how they affected history; health teachers can prepare a list of life-threatening diseases and ask students to rank order from most to least those that cause the most deaths in a certain target group; science teachers can prepare a list of pollution producers (e.g., cars, airplanes, industrial waste, consumer waste products) and rank order those that are the most to least guilty of adversely affecting the environment.

Figure 4.6: Cloze Procedure Preassessment

Cloze is a common strategy that is easily adapted for any subject area. For preassessments, I try to refrain from giving students too much support because I am curious about what they know as we approach a lesson or unit. However, you might give students hints by filling in some blanks for them to get their brains in gear. Or you can furnish a word bank if you think

Cloze Procedure Preassessment

Directions: Fill in the blanks with words you think make the most sense. If you would like to see a list of words as choices, let your teacher know. Otherwise, feel free to guess. This will not be graded.

The _____ coordinate system is formed by drawing two number lines that are _____ to each other and that intersect at their _____ points. This point of intersection is the origin of the _____ system.

The horizontal number _____ is the _____, with positive numbers to the right. The vertical _____ line is the _____, with positive numbers upward. The two number lines divide the coordinate system into four regions, called _____. Each point on the coordinate plane corresponds to a unique ordered _____.

Source: John Benson et al., *Gateways to Algebra and Geometry* (McDougal, Littell, 1993).

TEACHER RESOURCE

Terms

Teachers can provide struggling students with these words to use to fill in the blanks. Or, teachers might write words in some of the blanks so there are not as many to fill in.

rectangular	*x*-axis
perpendicular	number
zero	*y*-axis
coordinate	quadrants
line	pair

FIGURE 4.6

providing them with all the words is not too much support so that it deters you from gleaning information about what they know. The second part of the figure includes the completed cloze paragraph, the words if you want to use the word bank approach, as well as the completed cloze paragraph.

Figure 4.7: Analyze Fact or Fiction

In the book *Science Formative Assessment* by Page Keeley (2008), she introduces a strategy in which students defend or challenge a series of statements the teacher poses. "Through the process of defending or challenging scientific arguments aimed at the statements, students may solidify their own thinking, consider the alternative views of others, and modify their own thinking as new information replaces or becomes assimilated into their existing knowledge of beliefs." See Figure 4.7 for an adapted version of Keeley's science example. I modified how to use this strategy in the explanation that follows, although her basic premise of using it to encourage students to think about their own understanding and promote student inquiry remains. You can easily adapt the strategy to any content area by merely creating true and false statements based on what you are teaching.

- Students complete the sheet individually initially by reading each statement in the left-hand column and determining whether they agree, disagree, or are not sure about each statement and their thoughts. There is even an opportunity for students to write down whether the statement is contingent on something else by offering another choice: "it depends on _____."

- Teachers review what each student entered to preassess their current knowledge and level of conceptual thinking to inform instruction. From the information on the sheet, you can determine student grouping and design targeted readiness-based activities.

- Return their papers and have students work in designated differentiated groups to collaborate and research using a variety of resources at different levels of readability to determine the validity of the statements. Groups then agree on and enter information in the right-hand column—"How can you find out? What is the true statement? Explain why."—citing their sources and what they learned.

- Groups can present their discoveries to the whole class as students collectively gain new understandings from each other.

Figure 4.8: Informal Preassessment: Finger Symbols

Whereas the other preassessments are more formal and based on individual performance, this preassessment is informal. It calls on students to respond to line items using finger symbols to show what they do or do not know so teachers quickly get a sense of their impressions.

For this active participation strategy, present students with a sheet like "Informal Preassessment: Finger Symbols" geared to the content you

Analyze Fact or Fiction

Statement	How can you find out? What is the true statement? Explain why.
1. In the water cycle, water evaporates from Earth's surface into the atmosphere. ____ agree ____ disagree ____ not sure ____ it depends on _____ My thoughts:	
2. The water cycle renews Earth's supply of fresh water. ____ agree ____ disagree ____ not sure ____ it depends on _____ My thoughts:	
3. The energy that drives the water cycle comes from rain. ____ agree ____ disagree ____ not sure ____ it depends on _____ My thoughts:	
4. Most of Earth's water is available for human use. ____ agree ____ disagree ____ not sure ____ it depends on _____ My thoughts:	

FIGURE 4.7

are covering. For this example, it's figurative language. Teachers can include as many prompts as necessary to get a clear idea of students' understandings. To conduct this type of strategy, train kids how to respond and then throughout the year they will know the procedure. Here is how it goes:

- Tell students you will read them a prompt. They will then answer by holding up the appropriate number of fingers using the symbol key at the top of the page to indicate their responses. In Figure 4.8, one finger means the prompt is an example of "simile," two fingers means the prompt is an example of "personification," and so on. A fist always means "I am not sure." Tell students you are not grading their responses at all and this exercise is merely for you to know what they do or do not know. For visual learners, have the prompts visible for students to see as you read each one by displaying them on an overhead, a SMARTboard, or a document camera.

- Instruct them to signal with their fingers only after you have read the prompt, waited a few seconds for think time, and said the word "Show." Another point I mention to students is that they must hold up their fingers at chest level since it's a private communication between the two of you. I illustrate how holding up their fingers way in front of them or in the air would tip off others, and the point is for the teacher to know quickly what each student does or does not know.

- Quickly pan the room to get an idea of student responses. Sometimes I have to pan twice and say to kids, "I am going around the room again looking for responses because I haven't seen all people signaling. Remember that you can use a fist if you don't know the answer or are unsure." When you finish scanning the room, always tell students the correct response. Why? Because

Informal Preassessment: Finger Symbols

Simile: 1

Personification: 2

Both: 3

None: 4

Fist: "I am not sure."

1. Her words stabbed me like a bee.
2. The wind whispers in my ear like a small child.
3. Her eyes danced brightly like a crystal ball.
4. Her teeth were as white and straight as pearls strung neatly on a necklace.
5. Love is a floating cloud on which we carry memories.
6. Waves licked at the shore teasing the sand.
7. His nose dripped like a coffeemaker.
8. Tears are morning dew on the green grass, wet and glistening.

FIGURE 4.8

you have explicitly stated not to show others their fingers so they do not know the correct response unless you say, "Thank you. The correct response for the prompt is 1, a simile." Do not say, "Most of you got it right." That may be true that most students did in fact respond correctly, but if you are one of the few students who responded incorrectly, you might feel embarrassed or frustrated.

- This preassessment, like the others, can be easily adapted to use in other content-area classrooms. For example, in language arts, list three characters to use for the finger symbols and the routine fist for "I am not sure." Prepare quotes from the novel and have students match a quote to each character. In social studies, list three different historical figures or political parties as the possible answers for finger symbols. Provide different situations that match the figures or political parties. In math, list the operations as the basis for the answers and prepare several problems. Students determine which operation will help solve each particular math problem. In science, list selected geological time periods. Students match an organism to each time period.

Figure 4.9: Informal Preassessment Thumbs Up/Thumbs Down

Conduct this informal preassessment just as you would for finger signals in Figure 4.8. The only difference is that students are responding with "yes/true" with thumbs up and "no/false" with thumbs down. A fist always symbolizes "I am not sure." Answers for Figure 4.9: All are true except 3, 5, and 7. Here is what would make them true: In #3, replace *Hinduism* with *Islam*; in #5, replace *Buddhists* with *Muslims*; in #7, replace

Informal Preassessment: Thumbs Up/Thumbs Down

> Thumbs Up: true
>
> Thumbs Down: false
>
> Fist: "I am not sure."
>
> 1. Muslims believe that Muhammad was a prophet.
> 2. When Muslims pray, they face their holy city, Mecca.
> 3. Muhammad was a religious leader who brought the message of Hinduism.
> 4. Islam is a religion founded by Mohammed and follows the teachings of the Koran.
> 5. Those who follow the Islamic faith are called Buddhists.
> 6. The lives of nomads revolved around the seasons.
> 7. A pilgrimage is a journey to a market center where merchants sold their wares.
> 8. Muslims believe the Koran is the written record of God's words revealed.

FIGURE 4.9

Multiple Intelligence Preassessment

SAMPLE QUESTIONS

Multiple Intelligence Test for Children (ages 8 to 12)

1. I am good at copying what people say.
2. I really love books.
3. I really like to listen to the radio.
4. I really like to do "word searches" or crossword puzzles.
5. I really like language arts and social studies in school.
6. I really like to do experiments.
7. I really like math.
8. I really like science.
9. I am good at making and figuring out patterns.
10. I often wonder about how things work.
11. I am good at drawing or making things with clay.
12. I am good at learning new sports or dances.

Seven Intelligences Checklist (ages 13 to 18)

1. I easily remember memorable quotes or "sayings" and use them well in my conversation with others.
2. My library of books is among my most precious possessions.
3. I can hear words in my head before I read, speak, or write them down.
4. I get more out of listening to news on the radio and hearing books on cassette than I do from watching TV.
5. I am a master when it comes to word games like Scrabble or Password.
6. I enjoy entertaining others with tongue twisters, nonsense, rhymes, or puns.
7. Other people sometimes have to stop and ask me to explain the meanings of words I use in my writing and speaking.
8. English, social studies, and history are easier for me in school than math and science.
9. When I am traveling down a highway, I pay more attention to the words written on billboards than to the scenery.
10. I prefer social pastimes like Monopoly or other group games to individual recreations such as video games or solitaire.
11. I keep a personal diary or journal to record the events of my inner life.
12. I need to touch things in order to learn more about them.

FIGURE 4.10

Source: Adapted from the work of Spencer Barnard by Nancy Faris, graduate education student.

journey to marketplace with *journey to a sacred site.* This strategy, like the one featured in Figure 4.8, can be used with mostly any subject matter content. Teachers can issue these same informal assessments (Figures 4.8 and 4.9) to gauge how well students understand a skill or concept during the course of teaching a lesson. If used this way, it is a formative or ongoing assessment, and teachers would present as many prompts as necessary to get a pulse of student understanding.

Figure 4.10: Multiple Intelligence Preassessment

The Web site http://lth3.k12.il.us/rhampton/mi/mi.html provides a comprehensive explanation, examples, lesson ideas, and surveys for multiple intelligences. What is particularly advantageous about this site is the amount of survey choices you have to conduct with your students, or even take yourself, to further the work that you do in differentiation. Figure 4.10 features a sampling of some questions from the work of Spencer Barnard that his graduate student, Nancy Faris, adapted.

Formative Assessments

Typically, unit assessments have been seen as the project or exam that students complete at the end of a given unit and the only means for assessment. These summative assessments are highly effective and valuable in determining how well students have met standards and are progressing with grade-level work, but they are just one means of assessment. Formative—or ongoing—assessments can be considered routine tasks issued throughout the many lessons of a unit and intended for teachers to discover what students should know, understand, and be able to do. They provide teachers with essential feedback to inform their instruction all throughout a unit. Teachers can use the results, which are designed to check for understanding, to ensure that meaningful learning is taking place. Formative assessments help guide teachers in how best to accommodate student needs by gathering and evaluating data and using this information to effectively monitor and continue to design differentiated teaching opportunities. The assessments can determine if students are struggling and need additional support or require more of a challenge. Additionally, students can track their own progress and understanding as they review their performance on formative assessments.

Some formative assessments are more formal, while others are informal and give teachers a cursory look at how students are doing. While teaching various lessons, both types of formative assessment are used so teachers can recognize how students are faring and what they know and do not know. Formal ongoing assessments include items that students might hand in such as a written paragraph summarizing an article, notes or outlines, a homework assignment that is collected, quizzes, or a dialectical (or double-entry) journal. Assessments that are more informal include teacher observation of student participation in class discussion or small-group work, engagement in an informal student-teacher conversation, or choral responses to questions posed. You can use the finger symbol or thumbs up/thumbs down strategies introduced in Figures 4.8 and 4.9 as informal ways to check for understanding as well. Teachers use the results of formative assessments to monitor and adjust their teaching throughout the unit based on the results.

This section provides you with a multitude of formative assessment examples. Adapt, extend, and modify these examples as you see fit to

Read for Meaning

Clarifying	Understanding Concepts	Connecting
What were you confused by in the reading? How did you figure it out?	Draw a symbol or a picture of a quote or concept. Write the quote or concept under your symbol or picture.	Explain how a quote or concept you select connects with your life, other historical time periods, or the world today
Questioning	Comparing/ Contrasting	Predicting
Write questions that begin with *who, what, where, when, why,* and *how.* Answer any of them that you can.	Compare and contrast the actions of two characters in the novel	Predict the impact of a theme or concept from the novel on the world today. Or, predict what will happen next.
Guiding Question	Reacting	Summarizing
Select and respond to a guiding question.	Choose and react to some part of the chapter.	Provide a brief summary of what you learned in a selected chapter. Use only three sentences.

FIGURE 4.11

provide a host of ongoing assessments to check for understanding. Teachers who are most effective take the time to constantly appraise learning situations so they can adjust their teaching accordingly. Note: I use a heart symbol on tasks I prepare for approaching-grade-level students, a club or diamond for grade-level work, and a spade for high achievers. You will see these symbols on some figures.

Figure 4.11: Read for Meaning

After reading fiction or nonfiction text, have students complete "Read for Meaning." To differentiate this sheet by readiness, teachers can make three different copies and circle certain areas for different levels of learners to complete. For example, high achievers can make concept connections with the world at large. Struggling learners might be well served by teachers providing a concept with examples and asking students to create an accompanying illustration. After students complete their sheets, they can share their responses in a small group or with the whole class. You can also differentiate by assigning students to read different texts individually, in pairs, or in small groups based on readability levels or allow them to choose material based on topical interest. The "Read for Meaning" sheet is in response to these differentiated materials.

Figures 4.12 and 4.13: Graphic Organizers

An effective differentiation strategy is to provide students with a specific graphic organizer based on desired lesson goals. Teachers can differentiate by assigning the appropriate graphic organizer to students based on readiness so that struggling students have a modified version. Students can also choose the format that makes sense to them to organize their thoughts. In this way, it appeals to learning style as teachers make available several versions of graphic organizers or allow students to create their own. As a prewriting tool, graphic organizers help students formulate their thoughts coherently so they can write with a plan in mind. Students can also use them to identify the main points in a fiction or nonfiction reading selection or take notes while listening to a lecture, guest speaker, or video. In short, graphic organizers can be used as a prewriting tool and a way to organize content gleaned through reading or other means. They can be differentiated by readiness or learning style.

You can have students use graphic organizers to create a plotline of a short story they are assigned to write. But students can also fill in the organizer to reflect examples of plot elements for a story they have read or heard. Figure 4.12 requires students to identify the various elements of plot including a climax, which is a sophisticated skill for upper-elementary students. The alternate version, Figure 4.13, is more simplistic because it focuses on beginning, middle, and end. This is suitable for struggling middle school students and many upper-elementary students. For ninth graders and high achievers in other grades, ask them to create their own plot diagram that includes several conflicts and more sophisticated narrative elements.

Listed below are Web sites that offer graphic organizers to use for any assignment appropriate for such a tool: organizing thoughts, recording main points, comparing/contrasting, identifying cause/effect, concept mapping, and so forth. When perusing the Web sites, have your assignment clear in your mind, know how you want to differentiate (i.e., by readiness or learning style), and collect several versions to present to students based on learning and differentiation goals.

http://www.eduplace.com/graphicorganizer/

http://www.edhelper.com/teachers/graphic_organizers.htm

http://www.nvo.com/ecnewletter/graphicorganizers/

http://www.region15.org/curriculum/graphicorg.html

Graphic Organizer: Narrative 1

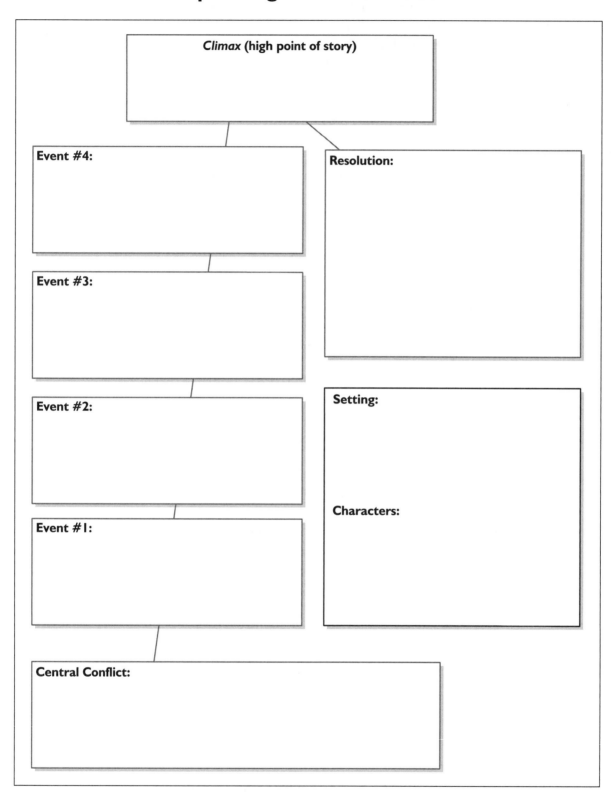

FIGURE 4.12

Graphic Organizer: Narrative 2

What characters are involved?		
What is the setting?		
WHAT HAPPENED?		
Beginning	Middle	End

FIGURE 4.13

Figures 4.14–4.18: Dialectical Journals

A dialectical journal is also called a double-entry journal. It is an opportunity for students to choose the part of a text that has struck them in some way and enter this excerpt in the left-hand side of a two-column chart. They then respond to this selected entry in various ways in the right column (see Figures 4.14 and 4.15). Or teachers might ask students to select or enter unit guiding questions in the left column and respond to them in the right column (see Figures 4.16, 4.17, and 4.18). It is a strategy for reading that allows students to connect with what they have read by self-selecting text or questions and thoughtfully responding.

Students can keep a dialectical journal in any subject area since it is used to respond to all types of reading. Science teachers can instruct students to respond to excerpts of newspaper articles or a video clip; social studies teachers can ask students to respond to a primary source document or textbook selection; math teachers can have students read a scenario that requires math skills and respond by explaining their approach to solving the problem; and language arts teachers can ask students to respond to a passage from a novel or short story or lines of poetry. Or teachers can direct students to select and respond to unit guiding questions. It would behoove teachers to model and specifically teach how to respond to the material selected or to the guiding questions when they first issue dialectical journals so students are aware of the criteria for what constitutes a meaningful and thorough response.

Often, teachers ask students to respond to text using a dialectical journal all year long to allow students time to reflect and analyze specific selections

Dialectical Journal: Historical or Nonfiction Text

Write Text Excerpt	Personal Response
In this column, write any words, phrases, sentences, or direct quotes from the text that interest you or confuse you. It is your choice what to include. Make sure you record the page number and the title of your entry so we can look in the text if we need more information.	In this column, respond to your entry from the left column. Choose one or more of these ways to respond: 1. Ask questions about historical figure(s) or event(s) and attempt to answer them; if you can't answer them, it is okay. 2. Make predictions about the outcome of a situation. 3. Analyze the text excerpt. 4. Draw a connection between what you read and other historical or current-day figures or events. 5. Comment on the terms used in the text in any way you want. 6. Make a personal observation about what you read.

FIGURE 4.14

Model for Dialectical Journal: History

Book: *A History of Us: From Colonies to Colonies,* Book 3, by Joy Hakim

Page: 42

Chapter: Nine, "A Girl Who Always Did Her Best"

Quotes	Personal Response
"Eliza Pickney played an important part in South Carolina's development."	**1. Questions:** Since it was unusual for women to be as successful in their own right as Eliza Pickney, how did others view her? Did she have any friends or were they fearful of befriending a woman who did not conduct herself like other women of her day? Did she run plantations all her life? How did she die and at what age? Who are outstanding women today who make a difference?
"It was a society of rank and class.... There were large landowners, and then merchants, craftspeople, farmers, indentured servants, and—at the very bottom—the slaves."	**4. Connection:** I wonder how far our current-day society has come from rank and class. There are still people today who are treated poorly because they do not have as good of a job as someone else or do not make as much money as someone else. And there are white supremacist groups who treat African Americans as badly as some slave owners treated slaves. In other countries, the mistreatment of persecuted people continues to rage.

FIGURE 4.15

or address guiding questions. It will not be the sole method of responding to text, though. For example, teachers might have students respond to oral prompts, complete a graphic organizer, perform a scene, facilitate a group discussion, and so on.

To orchestrate a dialectical journal as a comprehension strategy, teachers ask students to obtain a one-subject spiral notebook or designate a section of a three-ring binder. Typically, journal entries are assigned after a reading selection (e.g., chapter or chapter clusters, article or series of articles, selection from a document, etc.). Sometimes students are asked to write in class, and other times they are asked to complete an entry as a homework assignment. I tell students that journal entries must be neatly written and address the criteria by showing insight and thought. Although the quantity is not as important as the quality, I do not give students full credit for short, undeveloped responses and ask that they try again. If students have trouble responding, then tell them to rethink what quote or questions they selected in the left column that serves as the basis for their response.

Dialectical Journal: Literature Circles

Choose questions to respond to in preparation for tomorrow's meeting.	Respond to the questions you have chosen. Be sure to include the # of the questions.
☐ 1. *Point of View:* How does point of view shape readers' perceptions?	
☐ 2. *Plot:* How do events advance the plot?	
☐ 3. *Setting:* How does the setting play a role in the story?	
☐ 4. *Characters:* How are characters' internal conflicts important to the story?	
☐ 5. *Characters:* How and why do characters change over time?	
☐ 6. *Theme:* How does the theme of the story compare to other works?	
☐ 7. *Writer's Technique:* How does the author's writing enhance the story?	
☐ 8. *Author's Perspective:* How has the author's experience shaped this story?	
☐ 9. *Author's Perspective:* How does the author's message impact my views?	
☐ 10. *Personal Connection:* How does this story evoke personal connections?	
☐ 11. *Personal Connection:* How can you connect personally with any of the characters?	

FIGURE 4.16

Dialectical Journal: Religions of the World

Specific Religion: _____

Choose one or more questions.	Respond in detail to the question(s) you have chosen.
☐ 1. How did the evolution and spread of this religion affect communities?	
☐ 2. How was this religion able to spread and survive despite conflicts?	
☐ 3. How did this religion influence the social and political order in civilizations?	
☐ 4. How did ethical teachings and beliefs of this religion affect members of societies?	

FIGURE 4.17

There are several ways to differentiate a dialectical journal. Here are just some:

- Assign students different texts at various levels of readability as the basis for their dialectical journal response.
- Provide two or three levels of response choices. For example, instruct struggling students to make predictions, define terms, and ask questions. Expect higher-level students to analyze and critique their chosen quotes.
- Preselect and provide all levels of learners with specific quotes or lines from the text as the basis for response. This will help direct them to respond to passages that are appropriately challenging.
- At some point in the unit, all students should be expected to respond to all guiding questions since they serve as the basis for your conceptually based unit. You might, however, have high-achieving students respond to extension questions that have more depth and complexity as an adjunct to the unit guiding questions.

Figures 4.19–4.21: Categorization

This task calls on students to categorize items specific to a lesson goal. Each figure includes two tables: a club (♣) version for grade-level students and a heart (♥) version for struggling students. Teachers could make a third version (♠) using a spade symbol in which high-achieving students categorize more sophisticated terms, concepts, or attributes.

Dialectical Journal: Science

Choose a guiding question.	Write a detailed response.
☐ 1. How is electricity made?	
☐ 2. How do burning fuels provide energy for cars and electrical plants?	
☐ 3. How is the sun the source of multiple types of energy including the fuel that we use?	
☐ 4. What are specific renewable and nonrenewable energy technologies? How do they work?	
☐ 5. What are the differences between renewable and nonrenewable energy?	
☐ 6. How do renewable and nonrenewable energy benefit us?	

FIGURE 4.18

However, advanced students might have shown proficiency during a preassessment and do not participate in this formative assessment. In Figure 4.19, students categorize people, locations, and items associated with either Ancient China or Ancient India. In Figure 4.20, students categorize items into one of three groups: solids, liquids, or gases. And in Figure 4.21, students in language arts categorize sentences by how they begin (i.e., subject, adverb, or clause). Math teachers can create one asking for students to categorize word problems by the operation used to solve them. Foreign-language teachers can have students categorize words by topics (e.g., school, home, body parts). Struggling students are given the category titles for items they are to categorize. The grade-level and advanced students look at the items on the list, determine the categories, and then sort according to their established categories. In addition, struggling learners are given fewer words and phrases that are less advanced, but they still work to meet the goals of the lesson. These students work in small groups with the assistance of an adult if such a resource is available. An option for this activity is for teachers to cut out these words, phrases, or sentences and have students physically manipulate them into categories. This works well because it provides struggling students with a tactile activity and all students with a varied instructional activity.

Figure 4.22: Exit Cards

Teachers prepare content-specific or generic prompts that they issue to students during the last 3 to 5 minutes of class. These types of prompts—called exit cards—relate to the day's lesson, and students respond to them as a way for teachers to check for understanding and progress and for students to reflect upon key learning. Students can respond on index cards or scraps of paper. I use old library cards and paper from the recycle bin that I cut to a relatively uniform size. Ask students to put their names on their exit cards and collect them. Let them know that you are not grading the cards but will use them to help plan your teaching. After collection, sort the cards into three piles according to students' understanding: (1) students who are on target and clearly understand what is taught, (2) students who "kind of" get it, and (3) students who are clearly lost and need additional support. With this information, you can differentiate instruction by modifying or extending the subsequent lessons. Exit cards can be used on an ongoing basis as part of your routine or used on a periodic basis as you deem necessary. Some teachers call exit cards "tickets to leave" since students hand teachers their cards before leaving the classroom.

Figure 4.23: Informal Formative Assessment: Red, Yellow, Green

This strategy gives teachers instant feedback on how well students understand or do not understand a given task or teaching point. Prepare for this strategy by purchasing quantity sets of red, yellow, and green cups or

Categorization: Ancient Civilizations

♣ Arrange the following items into two categories. Give a title to each category.

• Siddhartha Gautama	• Four Noble Truths
• Confucius	• Himalayas
• People born within a caste system	• Buddhism
• Reincarnation	• Vedas
• Great Wall	• Early writing appeared on bones or bamboo strips
• Han Dynasty	• Hindu religion
• Indus River Valley	• Worshipped a supreme god, Shang Di
• Gupta Dynasty	• Invented paper
• Invented device for detecting earthquakes	

♥ Think about how to categorize the following items into two groups: Ancient China or Ancient India. Then write C next to items that correspond to Ancient China and I next to items that correspond to Ancient India.

Great Wall

Buddhism

Siddhartha Gautama

Confucius

People born within a caste system

Reincarnation

Early writing appeared on bones or bamboo strips

Hindu religion

FIGURE 4.19

strips of yellow, red, and green construction paper affixed with a metal ring to hold them together. If using cups, buy three packages of plastic cups each in these colors: red, yellow, and green. Buy enough cups so each student has one of each color. Distribute one set of red, yellow, and green cups or colored strips affixed with a metal ring to each student or group of students. After you present instructions for an assignment or sometime during teaching to gauge students' understanding, instruct students to stack their cups or show a colored strip to reflect their level of understanding: *Red:* "I am totally unclear and cannot move on without teacher assistance." *Yellow:* "I do have some questions, but I can keep working until the teacher is available." *Green:* "I am sailing along and can complete my assignment without the teacher's help." Show students Figure 4.23 so they are clear about how they are signaling. Use this strategy repeatedly so you can collect immediate data on students' level of understanding. With this feedback, you can attend to those students who need immediate support and also check in with those who

Categorization: Matter

♣ **Arrange the following items into two categories. Give a title to each category.**

1. Has neither definite volume nor definite shape
2. Coal
3. Composed of particles that move very rapidly and are at great distances from one another
4. Definite volume but an indefinite shape
5. Water
6. Helium
7. Iced tea
8. Particles are close together but can move past one another
9. Definite volume and definite shape
10. Gasoline
11. Particles are packed together in relatively fixed positions
12. Assumes the shape of its container
13. Quartz

♥ **Think about how you would categorize the following items into three groups: solid, liquid, gas. Then, write an S for SOLID, an L for LIQUID, or a G for GAS next to each line.**

1. Water
2. Definite volume and definite shape
3. Assumes the shape of its container
4. Quartz
5. Helium
6. Has neither definite volume nor definite shape
7. Coal
8. Definite volume but an indefinite shape
9. Iced tea

FIGURE 4.20

consistently show "green." Maybe the latter students are not being appropriately challenged, so attend to these students by differentiation.

Figure 4.24: Practice

A sound differentiation strategy that addresses readiness is to divide students into homogeneous groups and allow them the opportunity to practice a skill or concept together by grappling with and discussing a problem or prompt. Figure 4.24 shows a math example, but teachers of any discipline can create a table like this with varying levels of practice problems or

Categorization: Sentence Structure

♣ **Group these sentences into three categories based on sentence beginnings. Name each category to explain your grouping.**

1. We talked about politics and business.
2. When at last my own eyelids were so heavy with sleep that even my swirling brain couldn't keep them from closing, I could still hear the rise and fall of their voices.
3. If I had stayed any longer, my nerve might have deserted me.
4. Suddenly a shout resounded throughout the courtyard.
5. A dairyman with two pails yoked over his shoulders jostled me as I went by.
6. Obviously, you're poor, or you wouldn't have consented to travel as my servant.
7. If you don't keep quiet, I'll do as your mother suggested.
8. I'd never before washed myself anywhere but in the large wooden tub my mother placed in our courtyard or our room.
9. Slowly the caravan wound out of the khan's wide gate, down the street of the suq, and across the Thalatha Bridge.
10. Gindar nodded.

♥ **Think about how you would categorize these sentences into three groups based on how the sentences begin: *subject, adverb, clause*. Next to each line, write S for subject, A for adverb, or C for clause.**

1. We talked about politics and business.
2. When my eyelids were heavy with sleep, I could hear the rise and fall of their voices.
3. If I had stayed any longer, my nerve might have deserted me.
4. Suddenly a shout resounded throughout the courtyard.
5. A dairyman with two pails placed over his shoulders jostled me as I went by.
6. Obviously, you're poor, or you wouldn't have consented to travel as my servant.
7. If you don't keep quiet, I'll do as your mother suggested.
8. I had never before washed myself anywhere but in the large wooden tub my mother placed in our room.
9. Slowly the caravan wound out of the khan's wide gate, down the street of the suq, and across the Thalatha Bridge.

FIGURE 4.21

prompts. Copy the sheet onto cardstock or regular bond paper, laminate it, and cut out the squares. Distribute the appropriate problem or prompt to each small group for them to discuss and solve. If the practice is skill based, some students might not find as much benefit in this activity if each group shares with the whole class. They would, however, gain from hearing how groups solved problems or responded to prompts that are more conceptual in nature.

Exit Cards

Specific to content:

3—List three examples of nonrenewable energy.
2—List two ways that renewable energy benefits us.
1—Write one question you have about this topic.

3—Write down three subordinating conjunctions.
2—Write two dependent clauses.
1—Write one complex sentence.

- Write a quote that the protagonist in our novel might have said that the author did not include. Who would she or he say this to and why?
- Write a question you would ask the protagonist if she or he were here.

- Name two ways that you could use percentages in your life.
- Write a word problem using percentages and solve it.

- Identify two periods in history where this theme applies: "Intolerance leads to unspeakable actions."
- Explain how it applies to one or both of these historical events you identify.
- Write one question you have about what we are studying.

Generic prompts:

- What did you learn today that was new?
- What questions do you have about today's lesson?
- How can this lesson help you?
- What was the easiest task you did today? The hardest task?
- What made you really think?
- What did you like about working with a partner, alone, or in a group?
- How can you connect what you learned to something else?
- Was there anything that frustrated you?
- Was there something that made you feel successful today in your learning?

FIGURE 4.22

Figure 4.25: Blank Organizer

This blank organizer is my favorite as it can be used in many different ways as listed in the chart on p. 118. To differentiate, allow struggling students to fill in three squares, prepare an organizer for them

Informal Formative Assessment: Red, Yellow, Green

RED: Show red if you ...

- feel I have not explained this clearly;

- still have many questions;

- can't work without assistance; or

- do not understand what you are supposed to do.

YELLOW: Show yellow if you ...

- have a question;

- need some more information; or

- need more time to think.

GREEN: Show green if you ...

- really understand;

- can explain what you know to the class; or

- are okay if I call on you.

FIGURE 4.23

Practice

Create at least five story problems that use the addition of fractions and mixed numbers to solve them.	Write out the steps to the process of adding mixed numbers. Write neatly and explain each step clearly so others can follow your process.
Leo hikes 4 days straight. On Monday, he hikes 1¾ miles. On Tuesday, he hikes 5¼ miles. On Wednesday, he hikes 8²/₃ miles. On the last day, Bob hikes 10 ²/₅ miles. What is the total number of miles that he hikes?	Kimmie needs ¾ cup of flour to make chocolate chip cookies and 1³/₈ cups of flour to make a cake for the bake sale. She has 2¼ cups of flour. Does she have enough for the cookies and the cake?
Mr. Citrin donates $3 to Special Olympics for each lap that his daughter Sydney swims. She swims 28³/₅ laps in the morning and then another 30 ¼ laps later in the day. How much money does Mr. Citrin donate to Special Olympics?	Marshall goes to the beach boardwalk and buys 12 tickets. He uses ¼ of the tickets on a hotdog and soda. He uses ¹/₃ of the tickets on rides. How many tickets does he have left? How many more rides can he go on if each ride is 2 tickets?

FIGURE 4.24

that is partially completed, or allow students to complete the organizer with a partner. Assign the center box to students based on their ability levels so that all students are appropriately challenged in completing their organizers. Listed here are some ideas:

Center Box	Squares
Math answer	Four different ways to solve the problem
Vocabulary word	Synonym, symbol or picture, sentence, examples
Individual (politician, mathematician, scientist, history figure, etc.)	Personality trait, contribution, symbol or picture of contribution, today's effect of contribution
Concept (related to discipline: transportation, revolution, evolution, evaporation, etc.)	Choose 4: definition, present-day examples, historical examples, picture or symbol, effect of concept on the world, effect of concept on me, person or people associated with concept, evolution of concept

Formative or Summative Assessments

The examples that follow can be used for either formative or summative assessments. If used for formative assessments, consider them practice and a means to check for understanding so that teachers can guide their instruction accordingly. Summative assessments occur after a comprehensive unit of study to assess their complete understanding of the entire unit.

Blank Organizer

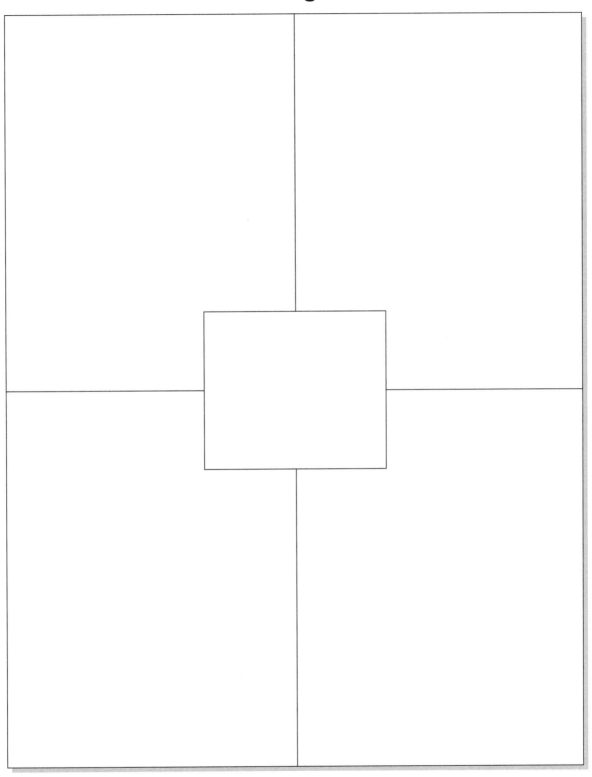

FIGURE 4.25

Figure 4.26: Assessments A to Z

These three pages include a number of ideas for formative *and* summative assessments that teachers can use in their curriculum to appeal to interest, learning style, and readiness. Following are just some of the many ways I might use them. When students are eligible for independent study because they have performed exceedingly well on a preassessment, I present these sheets and talk to them about a project they might like. Most times I will narrow down the list and present some of the choices by retyping them on a separate page or highlighting them on these actual sheets. When I create a RAFT (see Figure 4.27), I look at "Assessments A to Z" to determine various formats students can create. When I design lesson activities or projects, I refer to these sheets to provide a variety of different types of choices. Then, I create a criteria sheet for each or have students assist me in the criteria. I keep these sheets by my computer so they are readily available.

Figure 4.27: RAFT Examples

RAFT is an acronym: R for role, A for audience, F for format, and T for topic.

- *Role* involves these questions: *What role should the student assume? From whose point of view is the piece written?* For example, is the student assuming the role of a character in a novel, a historical figure, a scientist, or themselves?

- *Audience* answers this question: *Who will read, see, or use what I have written or created?*

- *Format* responds to this question: *What is the most effective and meaningful product format to show understanding of content?* This could be an advertisement, document, speech, skit, or clay model. Use "Assessments A to Z" in Figure 4.26 to see a list of format choices.

- *Topic* refers to the focus of the product. *What is the basis for this project, such as feelings about the war, explanation about the Periodic Table, or persuade to a position?*

In this type of assignment, teachers or students create choices for the role, audience, format, and topic based on content. Students then have a variety of ways to show their understanding of information presented. It can be used for any unit of instruction across the disciplines (see Figure 4.27), and the vast possibilities of what students can create make this strategy enticing for students and fruitful for teachers because it can really show depth of understanding in a nontraditional way.

RAFT can be differentiated by learning style if teachers or students create a variety of choices for format that appeal to how students like to learn. For example, a photo essay, newspaper article, interview, or three-dimensional model appeals to different types of learners. It can also be a readiness-based assessment if the choices for role, format, and topic are written at varying levels of difficulty. For example, a journal entry is less involved than an editorial. Also, the role can be more or less challenging based on the

Assessments A to Z

A

- advertisement for newspaper, TV, magazine, radio
- advice column
- allegory
- anagram
- anecdote
- animation
- annotated bibliography
- announcement
- anthem
- apparatus
- aquarium
- artifacts
- art gallery
- associations
- audiotapes
- autobiography

B
- baked goods
- banner
- batik
- bibliography
- billboard
- biography
- book
- book cover
- brochure
- building model
- bulletin board
- business letter
- business plan

C
- calendar
- campaign
- cartoons
- case history
- case study
- catalogue
- CD
- ceramics
- charades
- charts
- checklists
- clothing design—design or actual garment (historical renditions; current design)
- club bylaws
- code of ethics
- collage
- collection
- comedy (play; script)
- comic book
- community service or event
- computer program
- conference presentation
- convention program
- Cornell Notes
- costume
- course outline
- creation myth
- critique (written or oral)
- crossword puzzle

D
- dance
- data

E
- dance
- data
- debate
- demonstration
- design
- diagram
- dictionary with picture and words
- diorama
- directory
- display
- drama
- drawing
- editorial
- energy-saving device/plan
- equipment
- essay
- estimate
- etching
- eulogies
- exam
- experiment

F

- fabrics
- fact file on topic
- fairytale
- family tree
- fantasy or fictional story
- feature story
- flags
- flannel boards
- flip books
- formulas
- furniture
- future scenarios

G
- game
- gift
- glass cutting
- glossary
- graph with analysis
- graphic organizer

FIGURE 4.26 (Continued)

- graphics
- Greek myth
- greeting cards

H
- handbook
- headlines
- hieroglyphics
- historical fiction
- hologram
- "How To" paper

I
- icons
- iMovie
- index
- insignia
- instruments
- interviews
- inventions
- invitation (personal or business)

J
- jazz music or performance
- jewelry
- jigsaw puzzles
- job descriptions
- joke book
- journal (e.g., personal, historical accounts)
- justification

K
- kaleidoscope
- keepsake
- kit (e.g., survival, supplies, etc.)
- knitting

L
- labels
- lab experiment
- language dictionary
- laws for organization
- layout for building or room design
- learning centers
- lesson plan
- letter (personal or business)
- letter to the editor
- literary analysis
- lithograph
- lyrics

M
- machine
- magazine article or layout
- magic trick
- map
- mask
- meeting agenda
- menu
- mobile
- model
- monument
- multimedia project
- mural
- museum

N
- narrative
- newsletter
- newspaper
- news story
- notes
- notice
- novel

O
- oath
- obituary
- opera
- opinion
- oral responses
- organization bylaws, vision or mission statement
- origami
- outline

P
- painting
- pamphlet
- pantomime
- papier-mâché
- parody
- participation in whole-class or small-group discussion and activities
- patterns
- pennants
- performance program
- personal narrative
- persuasive paper or letter
- petition
- photo essay
- photograph
- pillow
- plan
- poem
- portfolio
- position statement
- poster

FIGURE 4.26 (Continued)

- PowerPoint presentation
- prediction
- press release
- project cube
- prototype
- puppet
- puppet show
- puzzle

Q-R

- quarterly report question
- questionnaire
- quilt (paper or cloth)
- quiz
- radio program
- reader's theater
- recipe
- research report or project
- response to literature essay
- résumé
- review of book, movie, experiment, presentation, etc.
- riddle
- role playing

S

- satire
- scrapbook (annotated)
- sculpture
- set/scenery
- short story
- silk screen
- simulation
- skit
- slogan
- song
- speech
- stained glass
- stencil
- store (layout, ads, purchasing, inventory, etc.)
- storyboard
- summary
- survey

T

- tape recording
- technology
- term paper
- terrarium
- test
- theme
- theory
- thesis statement
- tie-dyeing
- time line
- tool
- tour
- toy
- travelogue

U-V

- uniform
- unit of study
- vehicle
- Venn diagram
- verse
- vignette
- visual aid
- volunteer program

W-Y-Z

- walking tour
- wall hanging
- walking tour
- wall hanging
- watercolor
- weather map
- weaving
- WebQuest
- whittling
- wire sculpture
- woodcarving
- woodwork
- writing prompt responses
- written drama
- yearbook
- zoological projects

FIGURE 4.26

RAFT Examples

AMERICAN REVOLUTION

Role	Audience	Format	Topic
George Washington	Mother of a wounded soldier	Personal letter	Personal struggles
King George	Sons of Liberty	Document	Why independence is a bad idea
Patrick Henry	Tories or Neutralists	Propaganda	The fight for independence

RENAISSANCE

Role	Audience	Format	Topic
Chaucer	Readers	Poem	Story a traveler would tell
Saint Thomas Becket	Middle Ages citizens	Skit	Events leading to his assassination
European king	Peasants	Proclamation	Why taxing the common man is necessary

MATH

Role	Audience	Format	Topic
Store owner	Customers	Advertisement	All items 10% or 15% off
Baker	Customers	Window sign	Discounting some items 35% off and others 25% off
Restaurant owner	Dining customers who are senior citizens	Discounted menu	Entrees 20% off

POETRY: "THE ROAD NOT TAKEN" BY ROBERT FROST

Role	Audience	Format	Topic
Narrator	Self	Journal entry	Feelings about the path he chose to take and his rationale
Robert Frost	Readers	Magazine article	Explanation of why he wrote this poem and what it means to him
Student	Teacher/classmates	Literary critique	Analysis of the poem
Student	Teacher/classmates	Storyboard	Main ideas from the poem in words and pictures
Student	Teacher/classmates	Poetry sequel	What happens next in poetic form
Path not taken	Narrator	Monologue	Why he should have taken this alternate path

FIGURE 4.27

amount of available resources for the role the student is assuming as well as the types of resources. Figure 4.27 shows one table for a particular lesson or unit. It is easier to make one table for each lesson or unit where RAFT is used, but teachers can certainly create three different tables that represent differentiation by readiness or learning style. Then you can distribute the appropriate table to groups of students based on the type of differentiation.

Figure 4.28: Science Current Events

These checklists include a writing assignment for a summary of a science-related article. It can be differentiated by readiness and interest. Assign the appropriate checklist to students: The first page with the club and spade symbols is for grade-level and advanced students; the second page is the modified version that features a heart symbol. Allow students to choose an article of a topic that interests them as the basis for their written response. For struggling students, provide them with a few preselected choices of various topics that are at an appropriate level of readability.

Figure 4.29: A Personal Declaration of Independence

Teachers can instruct students to create a document modeled after an existing one. In this case, students create a personal declaration of independence using the same format as the Declaration of Independence. In other subject areas, there are written pieces that have a certain format like a lab write-up or a poem with a certain rhythm pattern. For the assignment in this figure, students choose the subject of their personal declaration, making it interest based. Conduct a class brainstorming session to provide students with a list of possible options for topics. Most students will state the obvious of what they will declare independence from, such as homework, chores, or siblings. Encourage them to include higher-level topics as well, such as to declare independence from homelessness, sickness, global warming, and so forth. Work with struggling students to outline what they might include in their personal declarations and allow them to choose any topic.

Figure 4.30: "She (or He) Is" Poem

Teachers can use this poem format in a variety of ways for different content areas. In a social studies classroom, the poem can be written from the point of view of a historical figure. I had students write it from the point of view of Eleanor of Aquitaine when they were reading *A Proud Taste for Scarlet and Miniver,* a historical novel tied to the Middle Ages. But they can also write from the point of view of a current or deceased political figure, mathematician, scientist, or themselves! (I even gave the template to my children and my nieces and nephews for them to write a poem to their grandfather for his big birthday titling it "Grandpa Is . . . .") To differentiate for readiness, teachers can dictate that students write a minimum number of lines, allow them to work with a partner, and provide a selection of choices for the subject of the poem. For example, give high achievers a list of individuals who require more research (for math, science,

♣ Science Current Events ♠

Assignment: I read a current scientific article and then type a three-paragraph paper based on the research findings. I use this checklist as a guide and satisfy each point.

Reading Checklist

☐ I find a **current article** that is no more than five months old from a magazine, science journal, newspaper, or the Internet that is of **interest** to me.

☐ The article focuses on one topic of **research** in **science or technology.**

☐ I choose an article that is **not too challenging to read**. That means, I might struggle with some words, but overall I understand the content and concepts.

☐ The article I find is **at least 10 paragraphs long.**

☐ I **read the article** and then **write a summary** using this checklist as a guide.

☐ I **photocopy the article and attach it** to my final summary.

Summary Checklist

Introductory Paragraph

☐ I provide the **title and source** of the article.

☐ I write the **main idea** of the article. This sentence focuses on the purpose of the article.

☐ I **identify individuals or organizations** who performed the research and **where** it was performed.

☐ I briefly **describe the research that was conducted.**

Body Paragraph: 2 quotes

☐ I **support the article's main point by including two quotes** from the article.

☐ I **explain what each quote means** in my own words.

☐ I include **additional specific details** that help my reader understand the importance of this research.

Concluding Paragraph

☐ I **write about how this research is important** by explaining how it could affect the world or help our understanding in a particular area of science.

☐ I include any **personal connections or thoughts.**

Conventions/Presentation

☐ I **type** my paper using **proper formatting:** 12-point type, Times New Roman or Arial, double-space, 1-inch margins, title.

☐ My paper is **free of grammar errors.**

☐ My paper is **free of convention errors:** punctuation, capitalization, and spelling.

FIGURE 4.28 (*Continued*)

♥ Science Current Events ♥

Assignment: I read a current scientific article and then write a paper based on the research findings. I use this checklist as a guide while writing and satisfy each point.

Reading Checklist

- ☐ I find a **current article** that is no more than five months old from a magazine, newspaper, or the Internet that is of **interest** to me.
- ☐ The article focuses on one topic of **research in science or technology**.
- ☐ I choose an article that is **not too challenging to read**. That means, I might struggle with some words, but overall I understand the content and concepts.
- ☐ The article I find is **at least 5 paragraphs long.**
- ☐ I **read the article** and then **write a summary** using this checklist as a guide.
- ☐ I **photocopy the article and attach it** to my final summary.

Summary Checklist

Introductory Paragraph: 5 sentences in length

- ☐ Sentence #1: I provide the **title and source** of the article.
- ☐ Sentence #2: I write the **main idea** of the article. This sentence focuses on the purpose of the article.
- ☐ Sentence #3: I **identify individuals or organizations** who performed the research and include **where** it was performed.
- ☐ Sentences #4 and #5: In the last two sentences of this paragraph, I briefly **describe the research that was conducted.**

Body Paragraph: Quote

- ☐ I **support the article's main point** by **including one quote** from the article.
- ☐ I **explain what this quote means** in my own words.
- ☐ I include **additional specific details** that help my reader understand the importance of this research.

Concluding Paragraph

- ☐ I **write about how this research is important** by explaining how it could affect the world or help our understanding in a particular area of science.

Conventions/Presentation

- ☐ I **type** my paper using **proper formatting:** 12-point type, Times New Roman or Arial, double-space, 1-inch margins, title. I may handwrite my paper and pay attention to neatness, spacing, and margins.
- ☐ My paper is **free of grammar errors.**
- ☐ My paper is **free of convention errors:** punctuation, capitalization, and spelling.

FIGURE 4.28

A Personal Declaration of Independence

STUDENT ASSIGNMENT SHEET

Due Date: _____

Create a situation in which you declare your independence from something, someone, or a group. This can be an actual situation or one that you make up. Write a declaration of independence for this situation that includes the following parts. As you write this, please begin each part with the titles used below (Part I, Part II, Part III, Part IV). Also, include a title for your personal declaration of independence.

Part I

Write an *introduction* that simply states from what you are declaring your independence.

Part II

State at least *four beliefs* about your issue. For instance, in the Declaration of Independence, some colonists' beliefs were the following:

- All men are created equal.
- God has given all men some basic rights, and these cannot be taken from them.
- Government should not be changed for small or unimportant reasons.

Part III

Explain what *wrongs* you feel have been done that have resulted in your declaring your independence. Include at least four wrongs. For instance, in the Declaration of Independence, some major wrongs included the following:

- The king did not let the colonists make all the laws they needed for their own good.
- The king taxed the colonists without letting them vote in Parliament on the taxes.
- The king would not let colonists trade with other countries.

Part IV

Finally, explain what *decisions* you have made to declare your independence from whatever or whomever. For instance, in the Declaration of Independence, the decisions included the following:

- "We say that these states are no longer under the rule of England and its king."
- "We, the representatives of the United States of America, by the power given to us by the people in these colonies, say that these united colonies are, and have the right to be, free and independent states."

FIGURE 4.29

or social studies) or who are more obscure characters (for literature). Give struggling students a list of individuals who are well known and have many resources that are easy to read to extrapolate information, or characters who are more prominent and are frequently featured in the targeted materials. To differentiate by interest, allow students to choose the subject of the poem that interests them. Options: Students can title the poem using the name of the individual or character, or they can mention the person within the context of the poem. Another alternative is for students to *not* mention the subject anywhere in the title or poem. Students present the poem to small groups or the whole class and their peers have to guess who the individual/character is based on the poem.

Summative Assessments

In the *Educational Leadership* article "Seven Practices for Effective Learning" by Jay McTighe and Ken O'Connor (2005), they provide this definition: "*Summative* assessments summarize what students have learned at the conclusion of an instructional segment. These assessments tend to be evaluative, and teachers typically encapsulate and report assessment results as a score or a grade." Examples of such assessments include final exams, a formal research paper scored against a genre-based rubric, a culminating project such as a 3-D model or a portfolio. Summative assessments alone, as McTighe and O'Connor (2005) state, "are insufficient tools for maximizing learning. Waiting until the end of a teaching period to find out how well students have learned is simply too late." In other words, although summative assessments are important, other types of assessments are equally valuable.

Summative assessments can be an end-of-the-unit test along with a cumulative project that both gauge how well students have met standards and the goals of a given unit. In this section, I provide several suggestions for summative assessments. Regardless of the discipline you teach, review these samples and see how the strategies might transfer to curriculum that you impart to your students.

Figures 4.31–4.33: Physics Project

This is an assignment differentiated by learning style in that students choose their own product to complete from among a list. It is also differentiated by readiness since students complete their chosen product against readiness-based criteria.

Figure 4.31 includes a series of checklists at three different ability levels reflecting the readiness-based criteria. The heart symbol (♥) represents the less intense option, the club symbol (♣) is the checklist for grade-level students, and the spade symbol (♠) is the checklist for high achievers. Teachers might have only a few students work with the heart and spade checklists, as a majority of the students might be well-served by the checklist with the club symbol.

Students choose a culminating product (Figure 4.32) and use their assigned checklist (Figure 4.31) as a guide to completing it. The list of

"She (or He) Is" Poem

Choose an individual as the focus for your poem. Your poem will begin and end with this line: *"She (or he) is"* followed by two personality traits. Remember that traits are expressed as adjectives, such as *persevering, tenacious, gullible, wise, cruel, innovative.*

In your poem, support these two personality traits with several lines beginning with *"She (he)"* followed by a verb. Below is a list of verbs that you might use, or create your own. Example: *She worries about the abuse of the environment.* Or *She assumes others know she was a pioneer in the field of radioactivity.* Or *She wishes others were aware of her innate sense of fairness.*

Write as many stanzas as you wish. Your poem does not have to rhyme, but it can if it doesn't sound forced or awkward. You will be assessed on the following:

- how well you follow these directions
- an appropriate and creative title
- the appropriateness of the personality traits to match the targeted individual
- the thoughtfulness, insight, and accuracy of each line to support the traits

wonders	dreams	believes
wishes	wants	strives
means to	hopes	realizes
waits for	decries	beholds
manages to	worries about	tries
aspires	loves	likes
cares for	dislikes	loathes
eats	creates	demonstrates
belongs to	captures	wrestles with
screams for	craves	acts like
smells	excels	invented
enforces	delights in	supports
assumes	feels	protests
pretends	expects	buys/purchases
is fascinated	gloats	specializes in

FIGURE 4.30

project choices represent a wide range of learning styles so students can select one that appeals to their preferred mode.

Teachers score the project based on the rubric in Figure 4.33. Since students will present their projects, the rubric includes scores for both content and presentation. You can convert the number grade to a letter grade by using the formula in Chapter 2's Figure 2.15 titled "The 4-6-8-10 Rule" devised by Vicki Spandel (2001) in her book *Creating Writers Through 6-Traits Writing Assessment and Instruction*.

Figures 4.34–4.35: Learning Style Projects

This assessment is differentiated based on readiness, interest, and learning style and can easily be tweaked to work with any unit. The one presented here is for a literature study. At the start of the unit, teachers present a list of books students may read by conducting a brief book talk. Students write down their first, second, and third book choices and submit this ranking to their teacher. Teachers use these rankings to assist them in assigning a book to each student. This method fosters interest but also readiness in that students choose a few books on their own, but teachers have the final say in the appropriate challenge level of the text. I also use this method when I present students with various topic choices knowing some are more challenging than others. I list the topics and have students choose the three that appeal to them most, and then I assign the appropriate one based on student ability. Topics that are more difficult represent those where little resources are found or the resources that are available are particularly more challenging than a more common topic. In this regard, these scenarios represent a type of controlled differentiation in that teachers allow students to choose what interests them but within a sphere of appropriately challenging readiness choices.

Early in the unit, teachers present Figure 4.34, which lists the milestones for the unit and a list of project choices with checklists and graphic organizers. During or near the end of the unit, students work on their selected projects. These projects are consciously designed by learning style so students have the potential to flourish by working in their preferred mode. Invite students to work individually or in pairs. Even though these projects are differentiated by learning style, teachers can certainly modify or extend any of the checklists or graphic organizers to meet a particular challenge level of individual learners. Also, allow any student to create and complete an alternate graphic organizer or project if what is provided does not meet his or her needs.

Figure 4.35 is the rubric for scoring the projects. To convert the number score to a letter grade, use the conversion factoring shown in Chapter 2's Figure 2.15, "The 4-6-8-10 Rule," developed by Vicki Spandel (2001) and featured in her book *Creating Writers Through 6-Traits Writing Assessment and Instruction*.

Figure 4.36: Tic-Tac-Toe

This figure shows a readiness-based differentiation strategy called Tic-Tac-Toe specifically for a study of the Crusades. Students choose three

(Text continues on p. 144.)

Summative Assessment: ♠ Physics Project Checklist

You will complete a project that shows your understanding of our previous unit on "Motion" and our current unit on "Forces." Specifically, I want you to demonstrate that you are knowledgeable about how unbalanced forces cause changes in velocity. To show your understanding, you will create a project of your choice from the sheet titled "Flying Physics Project Choices." Any project you choose must include the items on the checklist below to fully satisfy this project.

- ☐ I clearly define **velocity.**
- ☐ I provide an example of how average speed is calculated by showing the accurate **math formula.**
- ☐ I clearly define **force.**
- ☐ I clearly define **four forces of flight.**
- ☐ I draw or provide photographs for each of the **major parts of the airplane** that are involved in each of the four forces of flight. Each part is accompanied by a **caption that explains the function.**
- ☐ I include a definition and pictures to explain **Bernoulli's Principle.**
- ☐ I explain why decorating an airplane model **would interfere with its function.**
- ☐ I provide at least two examples of **two pairs of unbalanced forces interacting** to produce movement.
- ☐ I use **accurate terms.** I have checked all of my facts.
- ☐ My writing is typed and includes **proper grammar and conventions** (i.e., periods, capitalization, spelling, punctuation, indenting).
- ☐ My artwork/graphics are **colorful, detailed, creative, and neat.**
- ☐ My writing is organized in a way that makes sense, and all of my **main points are clearly identified by subheadings and titles.**
- ☐ My project has an **appropriate title** and my **name/class period.**
- ☐ It is obvious that I have done my **personal best.**

FIGURE 4.31 (*Continued*)

Summative Assessment: ♣ Physics Project Checklist

You will complete a project that shows your understanding of our previous unit on "Motion" and our current unit on "Forces." Specifically, I want you to demonstrate that you are knowledgeable about how unbalanced forces cause changes in velocity. To show your understanding, you will create a project of your choice from the sheet titled "Flying Physics Project Choices." Any project you choose must include the items on the checklist below to fully satisfy this project.

- ☐ I clearly **explain the difference between velocity and speed** and show an **example** of each. I include **math examples,** as appropriate.

- ☐ I clearly explain the **four forces of flight.**

- ☐ I draw or provide photographs for each of the **major parts of the airplane** that are involved in each of the four forces of flight. Each part is accompanied by a **caption that explains the function.**

- ☐ I include a definition and pictures to explain **Bernoulli's Principle.**

- ☐ I provide a **thorough and complete explanation** that accounts for why the same forces that keep a 747 flying also keep my SIOUX-Z-Q up and going.

- ☐ I provide at least two examples of **two pairs of unbalanced forces interacting** to produce movement.

- ☐ I use **accurate terms.** I have checked all of my facts.

- ☐ My writing is **typed** and includes **proper grammar and conventions** (i.e., capitalization, spelling, punctuation, indenting).

- ☐ My artwork/graphics are **colorful, detailed, creative,** and **neat.**

- ☐ My writing is **organized** in a way that makes sense, and all of my **main points are clearly identified by subheadings and titles.**

- ☐ My project has an **appropriate** title and my **name/class period.**

- ☐ It is obvious that I have done my **personal best.**

FIGURE 4.31 (Continued)

Summative Assessment: ♥ Physics Project Checklist

You will complete a project that shows your understanding of our previous unit on "Motion" and our current unit on "Forces." Specifically, I want you to demonstrate that you are knowledgeable about how unbalanced forces cause changes in velocity. To show your understanding, you will create a project of your choice from the sheet titled "Flying Physics Project Choices." Any project you choose must include the items on the checklist below to fully satisfy this project.

☐ I clearly define **velocity.**

☐ I clearly define **force.**

☐ I clearly define **four forces of flight.**

☐ I **explain** how I **reduce drag** on my airplane.

☐ I explain why decorating an airplane model would **interfere with its function.**

☐ I provide an example of **two pairs of unbalanced forces interacting** to produce movement.

☐ I use **accurate terms.** I have checked all of my facts.

☐ My writing is typed and includes **proper grammar and conventions** (i.e., capitalization, spelling, punctuation, indenting).

☐ My artwork/graphics are **colorful, detailed, creative, and neat.**

☐ My writing is **organized** in a way that makes sense, and all of my **main points are clearly identified by subheadings and titles.**

☐ My project has an **appropriate title** and my **name/class period.**

☐ It is obvious that I have done my **personal best.**

FIGURE 4.31

Summative Assessment: Physics Project Choices

To display your information, you may choose one of the project choices below. Make sure you satisfy each point on the "Physics Project Checklist," so use it as a guide while working on your project. You will present your project to the class.

- ## Project Cube or Mobile

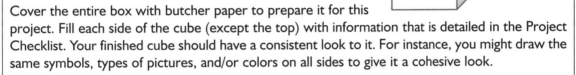

Create a project cube by using a mailing box with six sides.

Cover the entire box with butcher paper to prepare it for this project. Fill each side of the cube (except the top) with information that is detailed in the Project Checklist. Your finished cube should have a consistent look to it. For instance, you might draw the same symbols, types of pictures, and/or colors on all sides to give it a cohesive look.

- ## iMovie, PowerPoint, or Slide Show

Use technology to create your project. It must include all the information required on the Project Checklist. Time limit: 3 minutes.

- ## Picture Poster or Photo Journal

Create a picture poster in which you include all the information required on the Project Checklist. See your teacher for poster paper so the size is approved. Create a layout first and then use it as your guide before putting your work on the approved poster paper.

- ## Comic Book, Brochure, or Magazine

Create a comic book, brochure, or magazine that includes all the information required on the Project Checklist. Use a published comic book, brochure, or magazine as your guide for a layout. Attempt to make it as professional as you can.

- ## Song or Rap Song

Create lyrics to a song that includes all the information required on the Project Checklist. You might create a song from scratch by making up the melody and lyrics, or you might create lyrics to a familiar tune. Record the song on audio- or videotape and share it with the class. If you play an instrument, use it as you sing. Your song should have a chorus and at least three verses. Turn in a typed sheet of lyrics. Time limit: 3 minutes.

FIGURE 4.32

Summative Assessment: Physics Project Rubric

Points Attained		Project Feature	Criteria
Student	Teacher		
Content			
		Velocity definition	• Clearly defined; sophisticated = 10
		Force definition	• Clearly defined; appropriate = 8
			• Somewhat defined = 6
		Four forces of flight definition	• Unclear definition = 4
			• Inaccurate definition = 2
			• No definition = 0
		Reduce drag explanation	• Fully explained; sophisticated = 10
			• Explained = 8
		Explanation of how *decorating an airplane model would interfere with its function*	• Partially explained = 6
			• Poorly explained = 4
			• Inaccurate explanation = 2
			• No explanation = 0
		Example of *two pairs of unbalanced forces* interacting to produce movement	• Both pair examples fully explained; sophisticated = 10
			• Both pair examples explained = 8
			• One pair example explained; both pair examples somewhat explained = 6
			• Attempts examples; weak = 4
			• Inaccurate examples = 2
			• No examples = 0
		Accurate terms	• Consistently precise and accurate words throughout entire paper = 10
			• Most words carefully chosen and accurate = 8
			• Words sometimes carefully chosen and accurate = 6
			• Weak word choice and/or little accuracy = 4
			• Haphazardly chosen words = 2

FIGURE 4.33 (*Continued*)

Points Attained		Project Feature	Criteria
Student	Teacher		
Presentation			
		Writing is *typed*; project *neat*	• Very clean and clear; typed = 5 • Clean and clear; typed = 4 • Some messiness; typed = 3 • Messy and/or not typed = 2 • Unacceptably messy and/or not typed = 1
		Proper *grammar* and *conventions* (i.e., punctuation, capitalization, spelling, indenting)	• One to no errors = 5 • Two errors = 4 • Three errors = 3 • Four to six errors = 2 • More than seven errors = 1
		Writing *organized*; *main points clearly identified* with subheadings and title	• Writing is altogether organized; subheadings and title help the reader through the project = 5 • Writing generally organized; subheadings and title intact = 4 • Writing organized in some places; subheadings and title present, but may not help reader as much as they could = 3 • Writing disorganized in many places; little use of subheadings and/or title = 2 • Writing altogether disorganized; no subheadings/title = 1
		Artwork/graphics are colorful, detailed, and creative	Excellent = 5; Good = 4; Average = 3; Weak = 2; Little or no color, detail, creativity = 1
		Appropriate *title*; *name and class period*	• Title prominently and neatly displayed; name and class stated = 5 • Title neat; name and class stated = 4 • Title, name, or class missing = 3 • Title only or name/class only = 2 • Title, name, and class missing = 0
		Personal best	• Completely obvious that student did his/her personal best = 5 • Looks like student did his/her personal best = 4 • Some evidence of personal best = 3 • Little evidence of personal best = 2 • No evidence of personal best = 1

SCORE: ____ Content ____ Presentation

FIGURE 4.33

Project Choices With Checklists and Organizers

PROJECT MILESTONES AND DUE DATES

As you work on a project for your book, you are held accountable to the following milestones and due dates. You will work at home and in class to satisfy this time line:

MILESTONES	DUE DATE
1. **Select** three top **choices** for your **book.**	
2. **Review** the list and descriptions of project choices **and select one** that you will work on and complete.	
3. **Begin reading** the book in preparation for your project. Complete an appropriate graphic organizer that suits your project that you create.	
4. **Finish reading** and **get approval** from your teacher for your graphic organizer.	
5. Once you have gotten teacher approval, **begin working on your project**.	

PROJECT CHOICES

Descriptions, checklists, and graphic organizers of each of these projects are on the attached pages:

- Chapter Sequel
- Picture Poster
- TV Interview
- Project Cube

FIGURE 4.34 (*Continued*)

CHAPTER SEQUEL

Write a last chapter of your book. In this chapter, include character(s) and setting(s) that would make sense based on the novel. Use your imagination and make sure there is closure to the story. Include what you know about strong writing: word choice, details, proper conventions, and sentence fluency. Maintain the same point of view as the author did.

STUDENT CHECKLIST

- I show that *I have completed my reading*.
- It is clear that *I satisfy each point for my chosen project* from this checklist.
- I write a *final chapter to the book* I read that shows closure.
- The *characters and settings make sense* based on the rest of the book.
- I use *strong, descriptive words and phrases*.
- I include *specific and interesting details*.

- I *indent* where I should.
- I *vary my sentence structure*.
- I use the *same point of view as the author* did.
- I include a *creative title*.
- I include *proper grammar and conventions* (periods, capitalization, and punctuation). If I use dialogue, it is punctuated correctly.
- It is obvious that *I have done my personal best*.

CHAPTER SEQUEL GRAPHIC ORGANIZER

| What *characters* are involved? |
| What is the *setting*? |

WHAT HAPPENED?		
Beginning	Middle	End

FIGURE 4.34 (*Continued*)

PICTURE POSTER

Create a picture poster in which you create five drawings with captions for each drawing that represents five major aspects of your book. First, identify the five major aspects, such as one character, one setting, two events, and one vocabulary word *or* two characters, two settings, and one event. Create a poster layout in which you sketch drawings that represent these five aspects. Using your layout as a guide, draw finished pictures on your poster. Accompany each picture with a detailed, typed explanation. Remember to provide a title for your poster.

STUDENT CHECKLIST

- I show *I have completed my reading.*
- It is clear that *I satisfy each point for my chosen project* from this checklist.
- I *choose five aspects* about my book.
- I write an appropriate *title* that is artistically written.
- I *draw five pictures* that are detailed and neatly done about each aspect.

- Each picture is accompanied by a detailed *caption.*
- My captions include *proper grammar and conventions* (periods, capitalization, and punctuation).
- My overall project is *creatively done.*
- My project is done on a *regular-size poster.*
- It is obvious that *I have done my personal best.*

PICTURE POSTER GRAPHIC ORGANIZER

CIRCLE ASPECT: character setting event vocabulary SKETCH PICTURE: DRAFT CAPTION:	CIRCLE ASPECT: character setting event vocabulary SKETCH PICTURE: DRAFT CAPTION:

FIGURE 4.34 *(Continued)*

TV INTERVIEW

Create a script and then videotape or perform a live interview of a character featured in the book. Pretend a television personality is interviewing the person. Remember to introduce the person at the beginning of the television program and ask intriguing questions that would interest listeners. Reveal in the interview at least five important facets of this character. Have a friend or family member ask the interview questions while you assume the role of the figure. As you videotape or perform the program live in class, wear realistic clothes that this character would wear. Creativity is encouraged, such as including introductory music of the program, any necessary sound effects, pertinent commercials of the times, and so on.

STUDENT CHECKLIST

- I show *I have completed my reading.*
- It is clear that *I satisfy each point for my chosen project* from this checklist.
- I choose *one character* from the novel who is important enough to warrant an interview.
- I write a *script* between the interviewer and the interviewee focusing on five important aspects of this character's life. I include a *title for my script.*
- My script includes *at least five open-ended questions with detailed and accurate responses.*

- My script includes *proper grammar and conventions* (periods, capitalization, and punctuation).
- I present this script to the class live or through prerecorded videotape. I use *proper voice projection, eye contact, and gestures.*
- I wear *accurate clothing that depicts the character* when presenting.
- My *presentation is creative.*
- I use *note cards or memorize* my presentation.
- It is obvious that *I have done my personal best.*

TV INTERVIEW GRAPHIC ORGANIZER

Character: _____

Interview Questions	Character's Responses
1	
2	
3	
4	
5	
6 (optional)	

FIGURE 4.34 *(Continued)*

PROJECT CUBE

Create a project cube by using a mailing box with six sides. Cover the entire box with paper to prepare it for this project. Choose five aspects of the novel you read, such as one character, one setting, two events, and one vocabulary word *or* two characters, two settings, and one event. You determine the five aspects as you wish. Each side of the cube (except the top) will feature one structured paragraph with an appropriate title that supports the subtopic. Each paragraph is accompanied by a visual. Feature the book's title on one of the sides (except the top).

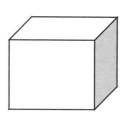

STUDENT CHECKLIST

- I show *I have completed my reading.*
- It is clear that *I satisfy each point for my chosen project* from this checklist.
- I choose *five subtopics* about my book.
- Each side of the cube includes an *informative paragraph and illustration about each subtopic.*
- My *paragraphs are organized:* topic sentence, support, ending sentence. All of my main points are clearly written.

- My *illustrations* are detailed, colorful, creative, and neatly done. Computer images are artistically displayed.
- I include a *title for each subtopic paragraph.*
- I include the book's *title* on one of the five sides.
- My writing includes *proper grammar and conventions* (periods, capitalization, and punctuation).
- My overall project cube is *creatively done.*
- It is obvious that *I have done my personal best.*

PROJECT CUBE GRAPHIC ORGANIZER

CIRCLE ASPECT: character setting event vocabulary SKETCH PICTURE: MAKE A LIST OF MAIN POINTS FOR PARAGRAPH:	CIRCLE ASPECT: character setting event vocabulary SKETCH PICTURE: MAKE A LIST OF MAIN POINTS FOR PARAGRAPH:

FIGURE 4.34

Project Rubric

	Components	Points
Idea Development/Content	**Follows Assignment:** completely follows assignment guidelines for the chosen project	• Assignment guidelines clearly followed = 5 • Assignment guidelines generally followed = 3 • Did not follow assignment guidelines = 1
	Quality of Content: fully developed; thoughtful, accurate, and significant details; shows knowledge about novel	• Fully developed and thoughtful; entirely accurate = 10 • Developed and accurate = 8 • Partially developed and thoughtful; somewhat accurate = 6 • Poorly developed; lacks thought; not accurate in many places = 4 • No development or accuracy = 2
Organization	**Overall Organization:** organized logically according to the requirements of the project selected	Excellent = 10; Good = 8; Average = 6; Weak = 4; No sense of organization = 2
	Title: appropriate title	Excellent = 5; Good = 4; Average = 3; Weak = 2; No title = 1
Conventions/Presentation	**Neatness/Visual Appeal:** overall neatness of project; legible penmanship; visually appealing	• Extremely neat, clear, attractive = 5 • Neat, clear, attractive = 4 • Some messiness; somewhat unappealing visually = 3 • Messy; visually unappealing = 2 • Unacceptably messy and unappealing = 1
	Grammar: sentences make sense grammatically (except for song/poem/interview)	No errors = 5; one error = 4; two to three errors = 3; four to six errors = 2; more than seven errors = 1
	Conventions: proper punctuation, capitalization, and spelling	No errors = 5; one error = 4; two to three errors = 3; four to six errors = 2; more than seven errors = 1
Voice	**Point of View:** paper written in appropriate and consistent point of view throughout	• Writer maintains consistent and appropriate point of view throughout = 5 • Writer might get off track once = 3 • Haphazard use of point of view = 1

FIGURE 4.35 (*Continued*)

	Components	Points
Sentence Fluency	**Sentence Beginnings:** includes a variety of sentence beginnings	• Thoughtful use of sentence beginning variety = 5 • Sometimes uses sentence beginning variety = 3 • All sentences begin in the same way by either the same word or the same type (e.g., all subjects) = 1
	Run-ons and Complete Sentences: includes complete sentences and no run-ons	• No run-ons; all complete sentences = 5 • Some run-ons or fragments = 3 • Unclear about sentence structure altogether = 1
Word Choice	**Vocabulary:** uses strong nouns, verbs, adjectives; no repetition	• Consistently precise, descriptive words; no repetition = 5 • Words sometimes carefully chosen and descriptive; minor repetition = 3 • Haphazardly chosen words; repetitious = 1

Student: _____

Highest Possible Points: 65

Total Points Attained: ____

Converted Letter Grade: ____

FIGURE 4.35

prompts on their assigned sheet that makes a tic-tac-toe win (i.e., three across, down, or diagonal). I have included three different versions. The heart symbol represents the less challenging version; the club symbol is for grade-level students; and the spade symbol shows a version for the high achievers. The impetus for the heart and club tables is from Pattie Drapeau's book *Differentiated Instruction: Making It Work* (2004). Tic-Tac-Toe is another strategy that can easily be adapted to other subject areas. Teachers can make one sheet with various projects that appeal to learning styles and invite students to choose what appeals to them. To differentiate by readiness, create three different tic-tac-toe sheets that each represent an appropriately challenging selection of project or prompt options for students to choose. My examples appeal to readiness and include written responses, but they call for student choice in the selection of prompts. I think it's best to provide choices whenever possible within a readiness, interest, or learning-style type of differentiation.

Tic-Tac-Toe

♥ **Crusades Tic-Tac-Toe**

How did the Crusades affect the Jewish people?	Describe a Crusader's point of view.	Crusade: Jihad: Persecution:
What was the purpose of the first Crusade of 1094?	Describe a trend in three Crusades.	What can we assume about the victims of the Crusades and why?
Describe the effects of the first Crusade.	Elaborate on your understanding of any Crusade.	Decide what would happen if you were involved in the Children's Crusade.

♣ **Crusades Tic-Tac-Toe**

How did the leaders of each Crusade differ in their beliefs and motives?	Compare three Crusaders' points of view with those of the people they encountered.	Create a metaphor to describe jihad.
What were the purposes of each Crusade?	Analyze trends in one Crusade to the next.	What can you assume about the followers of the Crusades?
Analyze the causes and effects of a particular Crusade.	Elaborate on your understanding of the victims of the Crusades.	What would happen if a particular Crusade were successful?

♠ **Crusades Tic-Tac-Toe**

Explain the presence and motivation behind anti-Semitism during the Crusades.	How did the Crusades impact international relations?	Why did Muslim and Christian soldiers join the Crusades?
Describe the far-reaching political impact of the Crusades that might have lasted into contemporary times.	Is there a parallel between the Crusades and the Islamic concept of jihad? How is there a parallel, or why is there not a parallel?	Describe the cultural impact of the Crusades on Europe.
Research a historical figure of the Crusades. Write a diary entry from his point of view defending his position.	Read and summarize in modern language a speech from the time of the Crusades.	Write an impassioned speech for or against a particular Crusade.

FIGURE 4.36

Comparison/Contrast Writing Checklist

Writing Assignment: You will write a comparison/contrast paper about _____ and _____.
Use this checklist to guide you while writing and satisfy each point.

IDEAS/CONTENT and ORGANIZATION

☐ I write a comparison/contrast paper focusing on **three aspects or topics about** _____ **and** _____.

☐ The writing clearly **addresses** all parts of the **assignment shown on this checklist.**

☐ I **indent** each paragraph appropriately.

☐ Each **paragraph** has **appropriate transitions** so the paper flows.

☐ I include an appropriate **title.**

➡ Introduction

☐ I **attract a reader's attention** so she or he wants to read more.

☐ I write a **thesis statement** at the end of my introductory paragraph that states each of my three topics.

➡ Three Body Paragraphs

☐ I write **at least three body paragraphs.** Each paragraph **focuses on a different topic.**

☐ Each of my three **body paragraphs is clearly structured**: topic sentence, support, and ending sentence.

☐ Each topic sentence for each paragraph represents a **main idea** that **supports the thesis statement.**

☐ I **support each main idea** with clearly stated facts, details, examples, and explanations from many sources.

☐ Each body paragraph is organized to suit comparison/contrast writing by stating **similarities and differences.**

➡ Conclusion

☐ My conclusion **sums up my best points** leaving the reader with a sense of closure. It is not too abrupt or long.

SENTENCE FLUENCY

☐ I write **complete sentences** so there are no fragments.

☐ I **avoid run-on sentences.**

☐ I consistently use a **variety of sentence types**: compound, complex, and simple sentences.

☐ I consistently use a **variety of sentence beginnings.**

☐ I include **appropriate transitions** to connect **sentences.**

WORD CHOICE

☐ I use **specific and accurate vocabulary suited to my topic.**

☐ My paper **does not include unclear language.**

CONVENTIONS

☐ **Spelling** is correct, even on more difficult words.

☐ **Punctuation** is accurate throughout paper and for the bibliography.

☐ I use **quotation marks** correctly when quoting sources.

☐ My **bibliography** is correctly formatted and reflects several sources.

☐ Appropriate words are **capitalized** correctly.

☐ **Grammar** is correct.

☐ My writing is **legible**, and my paper is **neat.**

VOICE

☐ I write in **third person point of view** throughout my paper.

☐ I know **to whom** (audience) I am writing and **why** (purpose) I am writing.

FIGURE 4.37

Comparison/Contrast Writing Rubric

	IDEAS AND CONTENT	ORGANIZATION	VOICE
5	• One clear, sophisticated main idea; stays on topic • All concrete and specific reasons/evidence for support; beyond grade level in sophistication • Many interesting and original reasons/evidence for support • Similarities and differences completely addressed; grade level or more above in sophistication • Writer is knowledgeable about topic and understands it well • Includes all parts of assignment; might even go beyond	• Clearly strong and sophisticated opening attracts reader • Strongly stated and sophisticated thesis • Thoughtful and sophisticated transitions connect main ideas between paragraphs • Clear and consistently structured body paragraphs: topic sentence, relevant/detailed support, concluding sentence (if needed); indents correctly and even creatively • Sequenced according to comparison/contrast writing • Effective and sophisticated ending gives closure	• Writer consistently maintains third person point of view throughout paper; no second person pronouns used ("you") • Clear sense of purpose and audience
4	• One clear, main idea; stays on topic • Concrete and specific reasons/evidence • Interesting reasons/evidence for support • Similarities and differences addressed • Writer understands topic • Addresses assignment requirements	• Opening attracts • Well-stated thesis • Appropriate transitions present to connect paragraphs • Each body paragraph structured; indents correctly • Sequenced according to comparison/contrast writing • Effective ending present	• Writer consistently maintains third person point of view throughout paper; no second person pronouns used ("you") • Clear sense of purpose and audience
3	• Generally stays on topic and develops a clear theme or message • Some concrete and specific reasons/evidence; some general	• Effective opening but does not create a strong sense of anticipation • Thesis stated, but lacks in strength	• Third person point of view used, although author might get off track just once

FIGURE 4.38 (*Continued*)

	IDEAS AND CONTENT	ORGANIZATION	VOICE
	• Some predictable supporting reasons/evidence; some original ones • Similarities and differences mostly addressed • Writer has some understanding of topic • Addresses assignment, but might miss a minor detail	• Transitions used and generally appropriate • All aspects of paragraphing usually correct; indenting correctly except for one minor error • Mostly sequenced according to comparison/contrast writing • Effective ending attempted	• Somewhat clear about purpose and audience
2	• Much of the text is repetitious and reads like a collection of disconnected thoughts • Minimal, general reasons/evidence; mostly listed • Predictable and sketchy reasons/evidence • Similarities and differences hardly addressed • Writer has little understanding of topic • Hardly addresses assignment	• Weak opening • Attempts thesis • Transitions used in some places; clearly missing in other places • Author unclear about a proper paragraph structure; little sense of indenting • Sequenced somewhat according to comparison/contrast writing • Weak ending	• Point of view off track more than once as writer changes point of view; second person point of view used • Unclear sense of purpose and audience
1	• Unfocused, completely off track; no identifiable point; length not adequate for development • Support is nonexistent, unclear, or trivial • Similarities and differences not addressed • Writer has no understanding of topic • Does not address assignment	• No sense of beginning • No thesis • No transitions or inappropriate transitions used • Lacks overall organization; paragraphing incorrect • Sequencing haphazard • Lacks an ending	• Writer has no sense of point of view • No idea of purpose and audience

FIGURE 4.38 (*Continued*)

Comparison/Contrast Writing Rubric

	WORD CHOICE	SENTENCE FLUENCY	CONVENTIONS
5	• Writer chooses consistently accurate subject-area vocabulary; vocabulary suits the subject and audience completely • No repetition, overly technical jargon, or vague language	• Writes all complete sentences; no run-ons • Uses sentence variety consistently: compound, complex, simple • Uses variety of sentence beginnings consistently, purposefully, and even creatively • Uses consistent, appropriate, and sophisticated transitions between sentences	• Spelling correct even on difficult words • Accurate punctuation, even creative, and guides reader through the text • Thorough understanding and consistent application of capitalization skills present • Grammar and usage correct and contribute to clarity and style • Altogether legible and neat
4	• Vocabulary is accurate and suits subject and audience • Little repetition, overly technical jargon, or vague language	• May have one fragment or one run-on • Usually uses a variety of sentence types • Most of the sentences have varied beginnings • Appropriate transitions usually used	• Spelling usually correct • Punctuation accurate • Capitalization accurate • Grammar and usage correct • Generally legible and neat
3	• Vocabulary is usually accurate and usually suits subject and audience • Might use some repetition, overly technical jargon, and/or vague language	• May have two fragments or run-ons • Sometimes uses sentence variety • Some variety in sentence beginnings • Some use of appropriate transitions; some are clearly missing	• Some words misspelled • Punctuation usually correct • Capitalization usually correct • Grammar and usage usually correct • Writing is somewhat legible; paper is somewhat neat

FIGURE 4.38 (*Continued*)

	WORD CHOICE	SENTENCE FLUENCY	CONVENTIONS
2	• Vocabulary rarely accurate and hardly suits subject and audience • Relies on repetition, technical jargon, and vague language	• Paper has many fragments and/or run-ons • Only simple and compound sentences • Little variety in sentence beginnings • Little understanding or usage of appropriate transitions to connect sentences	• Frequent spelling errors • Many punctuation errors • Many capitalization errors • Grammar and usage are often incorrect and contribute to lack of clarity and style • Illegible handwriting makes reader stumble; messy
1	• Inappropriate vocabulary for subject; does not suit subject and audience • Technical jargon and/or persistent redundancy distracts or misleads reader	• No sense of end punctuation or sentence structure • Only simple sentences or fragments • All sentences begin the same • Endless transitions or complete lack of them	• Writing too difficult to read and interpret due to numerous spelling errors • Punctuation is missing • Repeatedly uses capitals and lowercase letters incorrectly • Grammar and usage are almost always incorrect • Illegible; beyond messy; reader cannot decipher text

For papers that are completely off topic, score a 1 for Ideas/Content or a 1 for whole paper, as agreed among teachers at your grade level.

FIGURE 4.38

Figures 4.37–4.38: Comparison/Contrast

In this summative assessment, students choose a topic of interest as the basis for a comparison/contrast paper. It can be used in history to compare/contrast rulers or events, in language arts to compare/contrast characters, or in science to compare/contrast contributions of targeted scientific theories or topics. To modify, allow struggling students to write one or two body paragraphs. Teachers can meet with struggling students and discuss what line items to omit on the checklist (Figure 4.37). Score papers against the rubric provided (Figure 4.38) for grade level and advanced students. For struggling students, teachers omit some line items or columns to modify the assessment so it is in alignment with the modified checklist.

SUMMARY

Through pre- and formative assessments, teachers can make more informed decisions about how to guide instruction and differentiate for students appropriately based on the learning goals of a given lesson or unit. With the information that teachers glean in a preassessment, they can design differentiated learning tasks to meet the needs of students. Then, teachers keep track of individuals' progress and status by checking for understanding along the way in order to alter and adjust the tasks, as needed, and plan subsequent differentiated opportunities accordingly. As Douglas Fisher and Nancy Frey (2007) in *Checking for Understanding: Formative Assessment Techniques for Your Classroom* state: "Teachers need to use a wide variety of assessment systems (and regularly check our students' understanding) to know whether or not our instructional interventions, modifications, accommodations, and extensions are working." Designing, issuing, and assessing meaningful culminating opportunities—or summative assessments—for units are important for student learning, as well. They alone, however, do not maximize student learning; therefore, it is imperative that teachers issue several types of ongoing assessments if students are to have the full advantage of learning key material. All types of assessments need to be incorporated into curriculum as each works in concert with the other for a complete composite of student understanding and growth.

As teachers design their lessons, use the examples in this chapter and also in Chapter 1 to create appropriately differentiated assessments. Some lessons may not require a preassessment, but there could be ideas to flag for a unit preassessment so keep those sticky notes on hand. In Chapter 5, you will read about the lesson details; among them is teaching strategies. Refer back to the formative assessments in this chapter when writing step-by-step lessons because some formative assessments can double as teaching strategies depending on how they are used.

5

Additional Lesson-Planning Components for Differentiated Curriculum

Throughout this book, you have read and learned about several components of differentiated curriculum design. In Chapter 1, the focus was differentiated strategies; in Chapter 2, I introduced a lesson template and included several differentiated lessons for you to peruse; in Chapter 3, the importance of standards, concepts, and guiding questions as the foundation for any curriculum was the emphasis; and in Chapter 4, various assessments took center stage. In this chapter, I present the other lesson components from the lesson template that are essential to a well-rounded, effective differentiated curriculum. Specifically, the components include the resources that are needed, the estimated timing of the lesson (i.e., how long the lesson will last and when to conduct the lesson), and the lesson details, which represent the step-by-step narration of what teachers will do, say, and need to create and execute a lesson. It includes what activities constitute the lesson's focus, how students will be grouped, what teaching strategies you might use including ways to differentiate instruction, plus any extensions that make sense for the lesson's goals. Some teaching strategies listed here can double as formative assessments (see Chapter 4) depending on how teachers devise the lesson. Perusing this chapter along with others will serve to broaden your understanding and provide choices for how you can differentiate.

RESOURCES

Resources and materials consist of anything that you need to conduct a lesson or activity. This includes both student and teacher resources. If any new teacher or even a substitute were to pick up the lesson and look at the Resources list, she or he would have everything needed to teach the lesson or administer an assessment. It is like a baker who reads a recipe and looks at the ingredients. The ingredients listed are what the baker needs to be successful during the baking project. In a differentiated classroom, a teacher needs several resources to provide for the different ability levels, learning styles, and interests of students. For example, you might have two or three different versions of an activity assignment sheet, various biographies, lab materials for two different labs, and so forth. The following is an example of a Resource entry for a particular social studies lesson:

- "National Government" blank (provided)
- "National Government" answers (provided as teacher resource)
- "Words in the Preamble"—three different versions: ♠ for high achievers, ♣ for grade-level students, and ♥ for struggling learners (provided)
- "Preamble to the U.S. Constitution" (provided)
- "California Constitution Preamble" (provided)
- *History Alive! Pursuing American Ideals* (©2007) textbook, Chapter 6, "Creating a Constitution," and Chapter 7, "An Enduring Plan of Government"
- Dictionary; thesaurus
- Resources for three branches of government at varying levels of readability (e.g., textbooks, teacher resources, articles, videos, picture books, computer software, etc.)
- Videos through San Mateo Country Office of Education/Technology and Media Services Center:
  - "America Rock" V9939 (30 minutes)
  - "Our Constitution: The Doctor That Gave Birth to a Nation" V10607 (24 minutes)
  - "Rights and Responsibilities" V10061 (18 minutes)

In Figure 5.1, "General Resources," I've listed various options for resources that teachers might use for a given lesson or unit. In Figure 5.2, "Resource Examples for Core Curriculum," I've listed examples of resources geared to a specific content-area classroom. You can get even more detailed than what I have shown in Figure 5.2, and I encourage you

General Resources

Biographies	Magazine articles
Autobiographies	Newspaper articles
Short stories	Web sites
Novels	Computers/software
Diaries	LCD projector
Student journals	SMARTboard, document camera
Published journals	Artwork
Plays	Photographs
Graphic organizers	Music (CDs, cassette)
Reader's theater	Primary source documents
Literary analysis	Guest speakers
Speeches	Student handouts
Poems	Student checklists
Textbook	Rubrics
Videos	Teacher resources (e.g., Web sites, college textbooks, literature guides, etc.)
Librarian	
Media Specialist	

FIGURE 5.1

Resource Examples for Core Curriculum

Language Arts	Science
• Biographies	• Magazine articles (e.g., *American Science Journal*)
• Autobiographies	• Newspaper articles
• Short stories	• Journal articles
• Novels	• Web sites
• Diaries	• Software
• Student journals	• Artwork
• Plays	• Photographs
• Props	• Videos
• Reader's theater	• Documentaries
• Literary analysis	• Perishable lab materials (e.g., pig's intestine, frog, cow's eye)
• Speeches	• Test tubes, beakers, safety goggles
• Poems	• Student handout (e.g., "Physics" Student Checklist, Lab write-up student assignment sheet)
• Literature and grammar textbooks	
• Literature guides (e.g., Novel-Ties, Scholastic, etc.)	
• Videos	

FIGURE 5.2 *(Continued)*

• Grammar textbook • Books on tape • Music • Artwork • Genre-specific writing rubrics (e.g., response to literature, persuasive, etc.) • Field trip (e.g., play, location of a setting featured in literature, etc.)	• Periodic Table • Videos (e.g., Bill Nye the Science Guy: *Atoms/Motion*) • PowerPoint presentation • Field trip (e.g., weather station, nature preserve, wetlands, etc.) • Research materials
Math	**Social Studies**
• Math textbook • Math manipulatives • Individual whiteboards • Math journals • Software program (e.g., Geometry's Sketchpad, etc.) • Web site: http://songsforteaching.com/ • Protractor • Rulers • Tangrams • Geometric shapes • Scientific calculator • 2- and 3-dimensional figures • Bank statements • Stock reports • Data displays • Charts, graphs, tables, diagrams • Guest speaker (e.g., architect, engineer)	• Documentaries • Recorded speeches (e.g., Martin Luther King's "I Have a Dream") • Simulation (e.g., Interact materials at www.highsmith.com) • Primary source documents (e.g., Declaration of Independence, historical journal entries) • Guest speakers (e.g., Holocaust survivor, Dr. Spalding, etc.) • Field trip • Historical fiction • WebQuest for research project on Puritanism • Graphic organizers (e.g., Venn diagram, outlines, T-chart, etc.) • Magazines (e.g., *Time for Kids, Newsweek*, etc.) and newspapers • Maps, globes, atlas

FIGURE 5.2

to do so in lesson plans and capitalize on the ideas in this figure. There are a multitude of resource options, and teachers need to list everything they use in the "Resources/Materials" section for a particular lesson.

Whatever way you group students and differentiate, all resources and materials should be included. For example, you might expose the whole class to a resource opportunity and differentiate the activities that accompany the experience. For example, during a unit on the Holocaust, perhaps a survivor is invited to be a guest speaker, which is a beneficial resource. Write down the person's name next to the entry *Holocaust Guest Speaker*. If you conduct a unit on scientific inquiry, and each year you have a scientist from a local company speak to the class, then write *Dr. Innesbrook from BioGenetics*. Another whole-class resource is a field trip. If you take students to watch a performance of *Macbeth* or *Romeo and Juliet* during a unit on Shakespeare, then write the specific play and location. If you visit the wetlands, write it down along with the address and contact information.

Teachers frequently use handouts as a resource, and they are often differentiated. List the exact name of the handout you plan to assign whether it is a handout you copy from a source book or one that you generate. Include the title you have given the handout in the list of resources and write "provided" in parentheses alongside it so anyone using your lesson knows that it is something included and not something they need to find. For differentiated handouts, indicate which version to use for specific groups of students. As I have illustrated, I use a spade (♠) for high achievers, a club (♣) for students at grade level, and a heart (♥) for struggling students. If you create four versions, then add a diamond (♦). I like these symbols better than A, B, C, or 1, 2, 3, where students automatically rank themselves.

If journals are used routinely, record *student journals* in the Resource/Materials section. If social studies or science teachers expect students to use Cornell Notes as a regular method for notetaking, then record *Cornell Notes* in the resources section. If teachers use a Cornell Notes Web site as a reference to create a student handout that explains the method, then include the Web site and write "teacher resource" in parentheses. You can find various helpful Web sites by searching the Internet. These are just two among many that you will find: http://coe.jmu.edu/learningtoolbox/cornellnotes.html and http://www.bucks.edu/~specpop/Cornl-ex.htm. It is important to consider resources you have used to create or augment a lesson and give credit where it is due like for the Cornell Notes Web site or for Teacher Created Materials, Novel-Ties, or other published sources.

A librarian or media specialist might be a particular resource for a given lesson. For instance, if you expect students to complete a research report, you might contact the librarian and ask her to pull from the shelves a compilation of books at various levels of readability related to an overarching topic on, say, the American Revolution. If students are researching their own topics, then teachers can still list *librarian* in the resources column to confer with her on what is available in the library, and also list *various resource books* and *computer for Internet search.* A media specialist might teach students to browse the Internet for reliable sources or direct them on how to search the Internet with efficacy to target their searches.

If teachers expect students to read a particular novel, then list the novel and its author. Even listing the ISBN number is helpful since novel versions are paginated differently. Textbooks are a regularly used resource, so include the title of the textbook, the publisher, and the specific chapter or excerpt with page numbers. I suggest even including the copyright date since textbooks are updated continuously, and you want the lesson to reflect a specific textbook edition and corresponding page numbers.

In terms of materials, do not feel it is necessary to list basic school supplies like paper, pens, binder paper, and so forth. Do, however, list necessary materials for a particular lesson like butcher paper, markers, transparencies, and transparency pens. If you need technology for a lesson, then indicate LCD projector for a PowerPoint presentation, SMARTboard, document camera, or some other device needed that is not typically in your classroom.

Preparing differentiated lessons for readiness and for students' interests and learning styles involves relying on various resources. Taking the time to create various materials and to find the right resources is a challenge, as well as finding the funds to obtain those that need purchasing. Because it is important that you find just the right combination of resources for the whole class, small groups, and individuals, utilize public libraries, secondhand stores, Web sites (www.half.com sells books in great or even new condition at half or more off the retail price), and donations if you are on a tight budget. Since there are all sorts of resources teachers need to create (handouts), organize (a field trip), and obtain (a book), carefully consider the goals of particular lessons or the whole unit and provide the necessary resources to make each lesson fruitful, effective, and differentiated.

On a final note, remember to update your resources for a particular lesson or unit periodically. Resources abound and are constantly created, so you should rejuvenate the lesson or unit you teach by infusing it with new resources if they are available. For example, there might be a more recent article to use, an updated software program, or a new video that has become available since the last time you taught the material. Also consider the technological advances that are available, such as SMARTboards and document cameras. In short, there are many valuable resources that may not have been created or available when you first taught a particular lesson, so keep in mind ways to update your teaching (e.g., attending conferences, reading professional materials, talking to colleagues, etc.) so you can become current.

TIMING

It is helpful to record how much estimated time you think it will take to conduct a lesson. Not all teachers have the same time block available, so offering approximate timing can help with time management to allow teachers to prioritize lessons they want to teach. Be clear if the lesson might take one or two class periods, and even indicate the time of a class period, for example, 43 or 50 minutes. If teachers teach a double-period core class, then write: "two core class periods of 45 minutes each." Additionally, include at what point in the unit this lesson might fall or what prerequisites are required. For example, if the lesson is a prediction activity, it is important to write: "Conduct this lesson after students finish reading Chapter 2." Or, "Conduct this activity after students have mastered addition of fractions." The clearer you can be in terms of timing, the easier it will be to follow.

The estimated time is intended for most of the class. In a differentiated classroom, struggling learners will quite possibly need additional time. Advanced students might test out of a given lesson based on pre-assessment results, so they might be working independently on a project or move forward at a quicker pace than the estimated time indicates.

Allow for these scenarios since differentiation requires teachers to be flexible to suit students' needs.

SKILLS AND ACTIVITIES

Skills and activities are closely linked. The instructions for both begin with a directive by way of a verb and help to define what students should know and be able to do. They are written after teachers identify the targeted standards for a lesson and create guiding questions. Carol Tomlinson and Caroline Eidson (2003) define skills as "the actions students should be able to perform or demonstrate as the result of a lesson, a series of lessons, or a unit of study. There are many categories of skills important to student learning . . . *basic skills* (reading, writing, computing), *thinking skills* (synthesizing, summarizing, defending a point of view, examining evidence), *production skills* (planning, setting goals . . .), *skills of a discipline* (map reading in geography, recognizing tones in music, interpreting metaphorical language in language arts), and *social skills* (listening, emphasizing, considering multiple perspectives on an issue, taking turns)."

Skills can become activities when they are more specific or when the express purpose is to teach a skill as a means for understanding the essence of a standard or guiding question, which represents the lesson's goal. For example, *compare and contrast* or *graph* might be the primary purpose of a specific lesson; hence, the skills would be for students to demonstrate their ability to actually compare/contrast and graph. Activities are more specific, such as, *compare and contrast the different political views of leaders during various wars* or *create a graph that reflects the number of soldiers injured or killed in 20th-century wars*. Additionally, activities do not always necessitate that teachers teach the fundamentals of the skills, but, again, that depends on the goals of the lesson. For example, teachers might conduct an activity where students list the various usages for percentages. In this instance, the goal is not teaching the skill of *listing* in this activity but rather including listing as an effective way to begin a particular lesson. When teachers devise skills and activities, they need to ensure that the skills and activities lead to mastery of standards because that's the overriding purpose.

It is important when listing activities to avoid the nebulous "know" or "understand" verbs, which lack concreteness. Instead, identify specifically what students are expected to do, such as *critique a movie* or *design a model* or *evaluate the results of a graph*. To brainstorm activities that are part of your developed lessons, use the list of verbs in Figure 5.3, "Verbs Based on Bloom's Taxonomy," and also Figure 5.4, "Examples of Activities Associated With Guiding Questions." In this figure are several examples of activities aligned to guiding questions for core subject areas so you can see the connection between the questions and activities. Other examples are at the beginning of the sample lessons in Chapter 2 where there is a box titled "Skills/Activities" with a bulleted list that includes activities such as *discern differences between writing samples, find narrative and expository*

Verbs Based on Bloom's Taxonomy

Knowledge		Comprehension		Application	
alphabetize	quote	account	moderate	adopt	illustrate
arrange	recall	account for	offer	apply	interpret
check	recite	advance	outline	avail	make use of
choose	recognize	alter	paraphrase	calculate	manipulate
count	record	annotate	predict	capitalize on	map
define	repeat	associate	project	chart	mobilize
draw	reproduce	calculate	propose	complete	operate
find	reset	change	qualify	compute	practice
group	say	construe	rephrase	conduct	put in
hold	select	contemplate	report	consume	put to use
identify	show	contrive	restate	demonstrate	relate
know	site	convert	retell	devote	schedule
label	sort	describe	review	dramatize	sketch
list	spell	discuss	reword	employ	solve
locate	tabulate	estimate	scheme	examine	teach
match	tally	expand	spell out	exercise	try
memorize	tell	explain	submit	exert	use
name	touch	expound	substitute	exploit	utilize
offer	transfer	express	summarize	generate	wield
omit	underline	infer	transform	handle	write
pick	write	interpret	translate		
point to		locate	vary		

Analysis		Synthesis		Evaluation	
analyze	experiment	arrange	hypothesize	appraise	judge
appraise	explain	assemble	imagine	arbitrate	justify
audit	group	build	integrate	argue	measure
break down	identify	combine	invent	assess	prioritize
categorize	include	compile	manage	choose	rank
check	inspect	compose	organize	classify	rate
compare	investigate	conceive	plan	conclude	recommend
contrast	look into	conceptualize	prepare	critique	resolve
criticize	order	construct	prescribe	decide	score
debate	question	create	produce	determine	select
deduce	reason	design	propose	editorialize	test
defend	relate	develop	reorder	evaluate	verify
detect	screen	devise	reorganize	give opinion	weigh
diagram	search	forecast	role-play	grade	alternatives
differentiate	separate	formulate	specify		
discriminate	sequence	generalize	structure		
dissect	simplify	generate	synthesize		
distinguish	survey				
divide	test				
examine	uncover				

FIGURE 5.3

Examples of Activities Associated With Guiding Questions

Guiding Questions	Activities
Writing: How do writers craft an introduction for a response to literature paper?	• Identify the author and title of a selected literary piece. • Write a context for reading so readers are familiar with the literature. • Formulate a thesis statement.
Foreign Language: Why is word order important?	• Identify word order in English sentences by parts of speech. • Explain the difference in word order between English and Spanish sentences. • Manipulate cards of Spanish words and phrases to be in the right order. • Create Spanish sentences using proper word order.
History: How does social order impact how people live in a community?	• Identify the various social groups of people in Medieval Europe. • Compile a chart listing the social groups and their roles within the community. • Role-play situations among social groups. • Compare/contrast the way people lived in the Middle Ages with people of modern times in various communities. • Write a historical journal entry from the point of view of a person in one social class to another of the same or different social class that addresses the guiding question.
Science: How are oxygen and carbon dioxide exchanged in your lungs?	• Explain what happens in an air sac. • Draw a detailed diagram with captions to show the process of inhaling and exhaling.
Science: How does gravitational force keep planets in orbit around the sun and moons in orbit around the planets?	• Name the planets. • Define gravity. • Design and build a model that shows the relationship between gravitational force and orbit.
Math: How do people interpret and use ratios in different contexts to show the relative sizes of two quantities?	• Define ratios. • Identify different contexts where ratios are used to show the relative sizes of two quantities. • Tell a story that explains how batting averages involve ratios.

FIGURE 5.4

examples, and *write a setting using imagery.* See Figure 5.5 for cursory samples of modifying or extending activities to attain differentiation. This chapter, along with others in this book, will assist you in taking your brainstormed list of activities and creating the detail necessary for choreographed lessons that foster meaningful learning and differentiation.

Examples of Differentiated Activities Associated With Guiding Questions

Guiding Questions	Activities	Differentiation
Reading: How is the protagonist an effective and ineffective leader?	• Generate a list of effective and ineffective traits that leaders possess. • Rank the complete list of effective and ineffective traits. • Determine what traits Ulysses possesses.	Struggling learners: • Teachers provide a list of traits that students use for ranking; define some traits for them. High achievers: • Compare the traits Ulysses possesses with present-day leaders.
	• Provide support for each trait using concrete evidence from the text. • Arrive at a consensus about whether Ulysses is a more effective or ineffective leader.	Struggling learners: • Teacher preselects several excerpts from the book along with a list of traits; ask students to match traits with each excerpt.
	• Write an essay defending position with at least three body paragraphs. (individual)	Struggling learners: • Write an essay defending position. (allow partners) • Teacher modifies essay expectations to include at least two body paragraphs; assist students with thesis statement.
Math: How do people calculate given percentages of quantities?	• Calculate the tip customers give servers for a dinner bill. • Calculate the price of an item of clothing that is on sale by a certain percentage. • Calculate the interest earned in a savings account.	• Teacher prepares differentiated handouts at various levels of difficulty calling on students to calculate different percentages.
	• Create problems involving discounts, interest earned, and tips for classmates to solve.	• Classmates share the problems they generated with readiness-based peer groups.

FIGURE 5.5

STUDENT GROUPING

Flexibility in grouping students is a significant characteristic of differentiation. A differentiated classroom is fluid, and students will move in and out of groups. Students work alone, in pairs, in small groups, and as a whole class in response to readiness, interest, and learning style. There are times in a unit when teachers allow students to choose their own work groups and other times when teachers purposely design student work groups. Sometimes you will want to teach kids as a whole class; other times you will divide them into groups, pairs, or trios. It is imperative to understand the goals for a lesson or unit and the results of pre- and formative assessments in order to determine grouping.

Students who are grouped by readiness are challenged appropriately by peers instead of overwhelmed by classmates who are too far advanced or not challenged enough by those far less able. Susan Winebrenner (2001) in *Teaching Gifted Kids in the Regular Classroom* states: "When the task is drill-and-practice (math computation, studying for a recall-type test, answering comprehension questions . . .), and you have evidence that some students have mastered that material, place those kids together in their own group and assign them a more complex task. . . . For tasks that focus on critical thinking, the development of concepts and generalizations, or problem-based learning, placing gifted students in heterogeneous groups may be perfectly appropriate." At other times, teachers can organize groups based on interest enabling students who are in different social groups, but matched well for learning style or interest, to find a new respect and alliance for each other. Electively choosing partners helps students feel more in charge of their learning, which you can do on occasion.

Depending on the composition of the class and the type of differentiation you choose, it may work out that there are not equal numbers of students in each grouping. In a tiered assignment based on readiness, it will be unlikely that one-third of the class is working on an above-grade-level assignment, a third at grade level, and a third below grade level. In reality, it might be that one or two students are advanced and working independently, a group of four might be struggling and need more teacher assistance and modified work, and the majority of the class would represent a third group. In an assignment geared for interest, students will work in a variety of grouping configurations based on their interest levels of the topic choices.

In sum, sometimes there will be whole-group instruction, other times the class will be divided into an even number of students in groups, and other times there will be a combination of students working independently, in pairs, and in small groups. The decision about grouping will be based on the type of differentiation (interest, learning style, or readiness) that best meets the needs of students and the lesson and unit goals.

TEACHING STRATEGIES

How do you teach what you set out to accomplish in the guiding questions? What strategies can you use? How can the lessons be differentiated? Often teachers reuse the strategies they are comfortable with and know. "Teaching strategies," as defined in *The Parallel Curriculum: A Design to Develop High Potential and Challenge High-Ability Learners* by Carol Tomlinson et al. (2002), "are the methods teachers use to introduce, explain, demonstrate, model, coach, transfer, or assess in the classroom."

In this section, I introduce some ideas for strategies that might be familiar or new. Use them as appropriate to provide an enriching, differentiated curriculum along with assessment suggestions from Chapter 4 and the differentiation and learning-styles charts in Chapter 1. Use these strategy ideas at any point in the lesson that makes sense to achieve the intended goals of guiding students to achieve mastery of standards.

When you peruse these teaching strategies, you will find that some require preparation like copying, laminating, and cutting to make sets of cards or to create a game board. When you have to create materials for manipulatives, game boards, or other quantity items, parents can be a valuable resource. When I taught, there was a parent resource center in our school district, so I was fortunate to have parents assist me. If you don't have a similar type of arrangement, call on your classroom parents for their help in creating these teaching tools. As a parent of a middle schooler and a high schooler, I'm always eager to help, so your students' parents might be too. You might be surprised by the support you receive when they are asked.

Pick Out of a Hat

- Prepare various prompts or problems. You can even prepare different scenes from historical events or literature. Copy them onto cardstock, cut them out, and put them in a hat or box. Arrange students into pairs, trios, or foursomes. Instruct one student in a group to randomly choose a prompt and then share his or her response with group members. Then another student can choose a prompt and respond, and so on. As an alternative, teachers ask a student to choose a prompt out of the hat and read it to the whole class. Each group confers and discusses possible answers. After groups have had ample opportunity, they share their ideas with the whole class. Teachers can take this a step further and have the class discuss which group had the most insightful, creative, or extensive response.

- Figure 5.6, titled "Informal Response to Literature Prompts," features an example of various language arts prompts. They are not differentiated, but rather provide students with an opportunity to discuss responses in heterogeneous groups. If, however, students answered these same questions based on different books chosen by interest or assigned by readiness, then it would be differentiated. This exercise might serve a purpose in launching a new unit or lesson and getting students primed for an upcoming activity. Textbooks sometimes have several problems or prompts that can be used for this activity.

- To differentiate this strategy, create several prompts or problems at varying levels of difficulty and have students work in homogeneous groups. Assign each group an appropriate prompt(s) or problem(s). Teachers might color-code the cards for ease of use or put symbols

Informal Response to Literature Prompts

Who is your least favorite character? Explain your answer.	Explain what part of the book makes you particularly angry.
Tell about your favorite part of the book.	If this book were made into a movie, what actor would you cast to play the role of one character in particular?
Would you have wished for a different ending? If so, explain how you would have ended it.	On a scale of 1 to 5 with 5 as the highest, how would you rate this book? Why?
What part of the book confused you the most? How did you figure it out, or do you still have questions?	What did you think is the high point—or climax—of the novel?

FIGURE 5.6

on each card to distinguish between high achiever (♠), at grade level (♣), or approaching grade level (♥). Figure 4.24 features a math formative assessment that serves the same purpose as a teaching strategy. It is designed as a readiness-based differentiation exercise as students are assigned particular problems to solve by level of learner. When differentiating by readiness, students do not necessarily have to share with the whole class if all students would not benefit from the input of others in different groups. To help you decide, read the prompts or problems you selected and ascertain if it would be beneficial and even make sense for all students to hear responses.

- After students respond orally to these prompts or problems and profit from classmates' input, when needed, they can write in their journals. In this way, group interaction and class sharing, if conducted, become a springboard for writing or an opportunity for students to refine their ideas.

Concentration

Make pairs of cards, such as vocabulary word and definition, math problem and solution, element with symbol (Helium: He), completion of a statement, or character with quotes or traits. In pairs or trios, have students play Concentration in which they first turn all the cards facedown. One student at a time turns over two cards to see if there is a pair. If so, the student keeps the pair and can have another turn. If the student cannot find a pair, it is the next person's turn. Students play until there are no more cards on the "board." To differentiate by readiness, make different sets at various levels of complexity and provide each group with the appropriate set. Additionally, teachers can devise a game for high achievers in which students find a trio of cards that match as opposed to pairs. Students can also make sets of cards to administer to peers based on topics of interest. For struggling students, simplify the cards and allows students to turn all cards faceup and merely find the pairs. The element of memory required for Concentration might be a chore for these students and impede the real goal, which is finding a pair.

Find Partners/Group

- Make pairs of cards like the Concentration examples above. Distribute one card to each student and have all students walk around the room to find their partner. To differentiate, give each student a card based on his or her ability level so she or he is appropriately challenged when seeking a partner. Teachers can color-code cards so they know to whom to distribute each card. Additionally, tell students to seek out partners with their same color. I suggest only two colors so that students have an ample number of peers to circulate among to find a partner. If you have too many colors, the groups are too small.

- As an alternative, teachers can create a grouping of cards. For example, one group can include an overarching category term (example: *noun*) and associations (examples: *intrusion, abode, convulsion*). Teachers tell students that they are seeking a category term and examples so when they roam around the room, they have an idea of types of cards to seek. Eventually, four (or five) students should find each other. Other examples include concept words (example: *patterns, conflicts, immigration*) and associated examples, key individuals and their accomplishments or characteristics, and math solutions and various expressions or ways to solve problems. Some cards might require a phrase and not just a word. If you have a class of several struggling learners, differentiate by color-coding so that the overarching category terms are in a color and the associated words/phrases are in white. Plus, give the approaching-grade-level students less complicated words so they are comfortable seeking out group members. Once all students in a particular group have found each other, they are to verify that all cards create an association that makes sense. To culminate, each group stands in the front of the class with their cards in front of them to get final confirmation from the whole class that their grouping is correct.

Games

Version #1:

- Arrange students into heterogeneous groups of four. Strategically number each student in every group so that all the 1s are approaching grade level, the 2s and 3s are at grade level, and the 4s are high achievers. For smooth transitioning, prepare the groups in advance by writing names and associated numbers for students to see on an overheard, PowerPoint slide, SMARTboard, or butcher paper like the following example in this table:

Blue Group	Red Group	Yellow Group
1—Jose	1—Shelly	1—Katie Z.
2—Amy	2—Katie R.	2—Meagan
3—Shakira	3—John	3—Romeo
4—Samantha	4—Alfredo	4—Ling

- Pose a question to the whole class, but make it clear that only a designated group of students is to respond. Questions are differentiated by readiness. For example, say: "For this next question, all the 1s may respond. The first student who raises his or her hand who is a number 1 may answer." Then repeat with another question at a higher difficulty level for 2s, and so on. Basically, all students assigned the same number compete against each other at a time.

Distribute differentiated study guides to all students prior to the game so they can each prepare for questions at their appropriate levels. Conduct this game prior to a quiz or test. As an option, students may confer with their teammates before answering, but the designated student whose number is selected leads the discussion and provides the final answer for the group.

- *Note:* Be careful how much you use this strategy because if the same students are repeatedly assigned the same number, then students will catch on to your method. This will not be so swell if there are competition or superiority issues in your classroom, making for some discomfort. Or maybe not. You know your kids so just keep this in mind.

Version #2:

- *Game Board:* In Figure 5.7 is a game board that you can draw by hand on a larger sheet of construction paper and laminate, or go to a copy shop and enlarge this figure. Make enough game boards so there is one for a group of three or four students. If you draw a game board freehand, create as many spaces as you want. The more game spaces you have, the longer the game will take to play.

- *Game Marker:* Each student in a group uses an improvised "game marker" such as a pen cap, a ring, or a paper clip. Teachers can provide other markers, for instance, different-colored beads or small sticky notes in different colors.

- *Question Cards:* Teachers or students create the game question cards and signify the difficulty level of each card by stating if it's a 3-, 2-, or 1-point card. Needless to say, a 3-point card would represent content that is more challenging than a 1-pointer. Each point then signifies how many spaces forward on the game board a student moves his or her marker. This method eliminates the use of dice. Teachers or students can create question cards. If students create them, distribute Figure 5.8 to guide them. You can differentiate this exercise by allowing students to work in pairs to create cards. Also, distribute different resources based on readability from which students can extrapolate information for their clues.

- *Star Cards:* When students land on a star, they choose a Star Card. These cards include messages that allow students to move either forward or backwards. It is a bit like the Chance card in Monopoly where a player doesn't know if the card chosen is a bonus or sets you back. Create your own Star Cards for this game that would resonate with your students. Here are some that I have used: "A student was absent from class and you offered to help your fellow classmate learn material that he missed. Move forward 2 spaces." "A classmate dropped her 3-ring binder and all the papers were tossed everywhere. You helped her collect her papers so she could reorganize her binder. Move forward 2 spaces." "You procrastinated on a long-term project and turned in a project that did not show your personal best. Next time budget your time more wisely. Move back 3 spaces."

- *Rules:* Students can determine in their groups some specific rules of the game such as, Should there be a judge in the event that an answer is close but not exactly as listed on the card? Should different people read the question cards?

- *Differentiation:* This game can be differentiated by interest so that there are several sets of cards that relate to topics within a greater unit. For instance, in a science unit on the universe, there could be one set of cards on asteroids, comets, and meteors; another set on characteristics and movement patterns of the planets; and so forth. It can also be differentiated by readiness as students play the game in homogeneous groups based on the different levels of clues that teachers or students create and various resources students use to create their clues. Also, you can modify Figure 5.8 for struggling students when they create game cards. Make sure several students are creating game cards since you wouldn't want students to play the game with their own cards!

Who or What Am I?

Prepare cards with the names of literary characters, individuals (e.g., mathematician, scientist, famous person in history, etc.), or concepts or topics (revolution, immigration, patterns, similes, metaphor, planets, etc.). Affix a card to the back of each student without him or her seeing the character, individual, or concept. You can attach cards with safety pins, yarn using a necklace style, or tape. Students walk around the room and try to guess what is featured on the card by questioning others and receiving answers. Differentiate by strategically giving each student a card that is appropriately challenging. You can then color-code the cards so that half the class has blue cards for higher-level subjects and the other half has white or yellow cards. Instruct students to travel around the room and approach only those students whose cards match their color. If you color-code into several colors, students may not have enough people to circulate among; however, you can gauge if three or four colors are too many based on the number of students in your classroom. You could alter this exercise so that students do not walk around the room but rather meet in a group of four. Each student takes a turn asking group members questions to uncover the identity of the person or concept on his or her card. To differentiate, arrange groups by readiness and prepare or have students create sufficiently challenging cards.

Manipulatives

Prepare sets of words, phrases, or sentences for students to manipulate in a tactile fashion based on directions. Copy the text onto cardstock, laminate, and cut out the manipulatives. Make sure there are enough sets for

Game Board

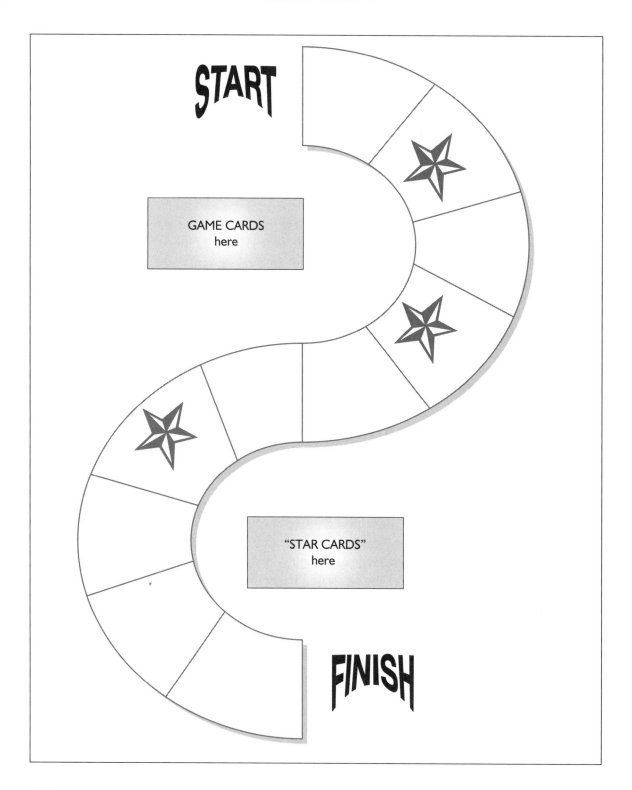

FIGURE 5.7

Game Cards

You will be making game cards with information you learn from our current unit of study. Use your textbook and other resources to create the questions and find answers for your game cards. You may work with a partner if you choose.

Use this checklist to guide you in creating game cards:

☐ Create *at least ten* game cards.

☐ Some game cards are to be *true/false*.

☐ Some game cards are to be *multiple choice*.

☐ Some game cards are to be *fill-in-the-blank*.

☐ Each game card is to be *neatly written or typed*.

☐ Write the *question on one side*.

☐ Write the *answer on the other side along with a point value* that represents the difficulty level of the question. Write "1 space" if the question is fairly easy; write "3 spaces" if it is a difficult question; write "2 spaces" if it is moderately challenging.

☐ All questions need to be *thoughtful*. All answers must be *correct*.

☐ Use *proper spelling and punctuation*.

FIGURE 5.8

each pair or small group. They can be differentiated by readiness so that groups are working with materials that are moderately challenging for their ability levels. You will need to spend time creating these sets, but you can use them year after year. Here are some ideas:

- *Sequence:* Prepare sentence strips for students to sequence, such as (a) the sequence of a story's plot, (b) the sequence of steps in the scientific process, or (c) the order of steps to solve a math problem.

- *Identify what does not belong:* (a) Prepare several sentence strips that show a topic sentence, supporting details, and extraneous details. Ask students to identify what details don't belong to make a coherent paragraph. (b) Prepare concept cards with examples and nonexamples; have students identify the nonexamples. (c) Provide a math property (e.g., Distributive) and several different kinds of number sentences that rely on various types of properties to solve them. Have students identify which math problems are not solved by the targeted property only.

- *Categorize:* Categorize words and phrases, such as (a) words according to parts of speech, (b) sentences that begin with certain words and phrases (e.g., dependent clauses, subjects, adverbs), (c) types of math problems that utilize the same operation, or (d) classification of living things. See Figures 4.19, 4.20, and 4.21, which can be used as manipulatives.

Gather Information

- Distribute one introspective question card to each student based on the current focus of study. Avoid questions that have a one-word response, but use unit guiding questions or create others that are thought-provoking. Students walk around the room and discuss questions and answers with three to five partners. Give a time limit of approximately two or three minutes for each pair to ask and answer each other's questions before calling "time" to find another partner.

- Debrief by holding a whole-class discussion. Then, students individually write a comprehensive answer to their question using the input they received from classmates and their own deliberations.

- Teachers can differentiate by assigning students specific questions. Struggling students might have difficulty responding to some questions issued to high achievers, so quietly let these students know they may choose to pass if asked a question that is too challenging. Chances are, though, students will gravitate to those who would be able to answer their questions.

- An alternative way to gather information in a kinesthetic and oral fashion is to have students walk around the room and find classmates who know specific answers to prompts. Once they determine that someone knows an answer, they must engage in a brief discussion, agree that the answer is correct, then obtain the classmate's signature. See Figure 5.9 for an example. The example shown is for social studies; however, the prompts can be easily adapted for any subject area. As you can see, there are several prompts. Students have to approach a different student for each box, so during the activity each pupil will interface with nine classmates in the example for Figure 5.9. It is not as profound of a discussion as responding to the prompts outlined in the bullets above because some questions are discrete facts, but it is still an interesting instructional strategy that students enjoy. To differentiate, you could make several versions of sheets. If students approach others who cannot answer a question, it is incumbent on them to find the answer through the textbook or other materials you have available. In this way, the sheet can serve as a study guide for an upcoming test. You might also have students generate a sheet modeled after the example.

Find a Classmate Who ...

Directions: Approach nine different classmates, one at a time, and ask each one if he or she can carry out the activity in a particular box. If a classmate can perform this task, have this person sign his or her name on the line in the box.

can explain what isolated China from other early civilizations. _____	can define cultivation. _____	can name the two major rivers of China. _____
can explain how oracle bones were used. _____	can draw a tributary. _____	can name the reason the Zhou Dynasty declined. _____
can tell you two new words he or she learned from this unit. _____	can draw a symbol for *cavalry*. _____	can explain *dynasty*. _____

FIGURE 5.9

Think-Pair-Share

The Think-Pair-Share strategy (Lyman, 1992) includes a systematic way for students to think about prompts that teachers pose in a way that elicits insightful responses. It includes the following three steps: (1) *Think:* Students individually think of answers to a question, problem, or scenario the teacher poses. (2) *Pair:* Students share their thoughts with a partner. (3) *Share:* Partners share their insights with the whole class. Often the verbal or more eager students shout out responses without giving others time to ponder their own thinking. This strategy allows ample time for individual thought so when students pair up, they each make valuable contributions and generate other responses together. During sharing, teachers record salient points on a brainstormed list or merely facilitate a class discussion based on the highlights of pair discussion. This can be differentiated by readiness as teachers assign different prompts to each pair.

Roundtable

You can use the Roundtable strategy (Kagan, 1994) in several ways: (a) *Preview* kids about upcoming content to see what they know; (b) *check for students' understanding* during lessons throughout the unit; and (c) *review* before a test to gauge how prepared students are to take the exam. Teachers review the number and quality of entries each student makes, along with observation, to plan instruction.

- I created Figures 5.10 and 5.11 for students as directions on how Roundtable is conducted and for teachers to understand the steps in the strategy. "What Do You Know About . . . " (Figure 5.10) is designed for you to use before a series of lessons or the whole unit. "Let's Review" (Figure 5.11) is used when you want to review information to check for understanding, which then functions as a formative assessment. Both activities are conducted in the same way. Students pass one sheet of paper around in a circle many times. Each time a student receives the sheet, she or he enters a word or phrase pertaining to the topic, being careful to avoid duplications. Give students permission to "pass" if they are finished contributing all they can. But encourage students to pass only after they have made several entries.

- Since this is a group activity for three to five kids, you may ask each student to put his or her initials in parentheses next to each entry made. Also ask students to write their full names at the top of the paper so you can associate the initials with specific students.

- When groups finish, have each group report their responses and post them on butcher paper. Remind students to read what is on the butcher paper before sharing so there are no duplications. Even though groups report their responses, still collect each group's list so you can see the amount and quality of entries each individual student makes. This will give you an indication of what they gleaned if Roundtable is done for the purpose of checking for understanding or review. If it's used for a preview, you can use the information as an informal preassessment.

- During a test review or checking for understanding, sometimes students like to compete in groups to see who has contributed more. I give the kids a time limit and tell them to keep passing the paper around until no more entries can be made. Groups like to see how many entries they wrote in comparison to other groups.

- The Roundtable strategy is helpful for differentiation. It can inform you about what students know prior to teaching so you can make decisions about how to differentiate for certain students. It is also another way to adjust teaching during the lesson or unit, as needed. However, note that all entries students make do not reflect a complete list of what they know since the strategy encourages no duplications. It could be that a student might have thought to record information but didn't because it was already listed. Also, carefully observe students as they work on this activity because you can glean information about how students participate, such as those who pass frequently or those who eagerly want to contribute line items.

Jigsaw

Jigsaw (Aronson, 1978; Clarke, 1994; Slavin, 1994) is a strategy involving two parts. First, students read material in a group to become "experts" on particular subject matter. They then form an entirely different group and share or teach what they each learned with others. To differentiate, groups of students can be assigned different reading material based on their readiness level or subjects of interest within a greater unit focus.

- *Group #1:* Teachers arrange students in initial groups based on the complexity of reading materials or areas of interest. Teachers should not feel they need to assign each group equal parts or the same kind of reading. If Jigsaw appeals to readiness, some groups are assigned less material that is comfortably accessible, while others are given more material that is at a more sophisticated and challenging level. For readiness or interest-based differentiation, it is perfectly fine to assign different types of materials to each group. For example, some groups read an excerpt from a nonfiction textbook, others read a magazine article, and still others might read a newspaper clipping or listen to a video clip or audiotape. But for interest-based differentiation, remember to allow students to choose their subtopics. After the materials are distributed or selected, students read silently or aloud (or listen with headsets). Tell them their task at the end of the reading (or listening) is to share their impressions of the main points with

What Do You Know About . . . ?

1. Take out one piece of paper per group.

2. Each group member is to have a pen or pencil.

3. Raise your hand if your birthday is closest to _____. You are first. The person on your left is second so that the paper moves clockwise.

4. Starting with the first person, write down one word or phrase that you know about _____.

5. Each group member continues to pass the paper around entering one word or phrase about what she or he knows about the topic.

6. No duplications are allowed, so read all the previous entries before writing yours. You are entitled to pass when the paper comes to you.

Time limit: _____.

FIGURE 5.10

Let's Review

1. Take out one piece of paper per group.

2. Each group member is to have a pen or pencil.

3. Raise your hand if your birthday is closest to _____. You are first. The person on your left is second so that the paper moves clockwise.

4. Starting with the first person, write down one word or phrase that you learned about _____.

5. Each group member continues to pass the paper around entering one word or phrase about what was learned.

6. No duplications are allowed, so read all the previous entries before writing yours. You are entitled to pass when the paper comes to you.

Time limit: _____.

FIGURE 5.11

group members. After reading, students discuss and clarify what they learned and then arrive at a group consensus about the five most salient points. Each person from the group records these five main points onto "Notetaking Sheet for Reading Group" (Figure 5.12). This group is sometimes called the "expert" group since students focus on being well versed about the content of their assigned materials.

- *Group #2:* Students form different groups comprised of one or two individuals from the initial "expert" group. Their job is to each teach others in their new group what they have gleaned from their materials using their "Notetaking Sheet for Reading Group" sheet. Emphasize that they are not to read directly from the sheet but rather use it as a guide to explain what they have learned. Students may ask questions for clarification, and you might expect them to take notes based on what classmates have explained and taught them. At the end of the exercise, students are exposed to information from different sources to see various perspectives, or they learn further about a subtopic that excites their classmates. Teachers may end the exercise with a journal write so students can share what they each personally learned and how it affected them.

- *Alternative:* The first groups stay together instead of reforming a second group. Each initial group shares its five most important points with the whole class. As the class listens, they take notes on the main points and include any questions they may have on "Notetaking Sheet for Audience" (Figure 5.13). The group who has presented answers any questions the audience might pose. Teachers lead a discussion after group presentations to debrief about the overall themes and concepts of the reading.

What's the Rule?

- On the whiteboard or overhead, make a two-column chart. Label one column "A" and the other column "B" like this:

A	B
•	•

- Say to students: "I will enter words (or numbers) in both columns and your job is to try and figure out the rule for why I placed items in the A column."

- Enter words (or numbers) one at a time back and forth from Column A to Column B. Pause after each entry and ask students: "What is the rule that accounts for the entries in the A column? In other words, what do all the entries in the A column have in common?" Enter as

Notetaking Sheet for Reading Group

Title of Your Assigned Reading: _____

List the 3 to 5 Most Important Points
1.
2.
3.
4.
5.

FIGURE 5.12

Notetaking Sheet for Audience

Topic:_____

5 Most Important Points	Questions
1.	
2.	
3.	
4.	
5.	

FIGURE 5.13

many line items as it takes for participants to guess what the A column words (or numbers) have in common. The B column entries do not have to have anything in common; they are random entries. The point is that the A column entries all have a commonality.

- Here is a math example (A = ways to express *one-quarter*):

A	B
• 1/4	• 13
• .25	• 50%
• 4/16	• .90
• 25/100	• 200/650
• 120/480	• 10/200
• 25%	

- Here is a Spanish example (A = things found *inside a home*):

A	B
• la cama	• la sierra
• la silla	• la escalera
• la lampara	• el carro
• el sofa	• los arboles
• la alfombra	• el tobogan

- Here is an example for science (A = *terrestrial environments*):

A	B
• rain forest	• coral reefs
• tundra	• oceans
• desert	• animals
• arctic	• forest
• grasslands	

- Here is an example for a parts-of-speech lesson (A = *nouns*):

A	B
• house	• run
• Dr. Smith	• hopping
• game	• naturally
• almonds	• as
• oranges	
• sweater	
• immigration	

EXTENSIONS

Often students are intrigued about a particular topic within a unit study and long to explore it further. Teachers who make opportunities available for their students at any time throughout the unit to continue to learn about what interests them on a deeper level have created what are called extensions. As written in *The Parallel Curriculum* (Tomlinson et al., 2002), "They may be of short duration (e.g., working with an interactive Web site or listening to a community speaker) or may require more extensive time (e.g., conducting an independent study, participating in a Web quest, or staging a performance)." Since extensions originate with content presented in class, make sure the activities relate to the key concepts and are not arbitrary or random exercises. To help you create extension activities, you might rely on others such as media specialists, librarians, content specialists in the field, or colleagues. Students can even volunteer with or shadow a professional who works in a particular vocation. To this point, extension activities can take place in an authentic setting such as a workplace, in the classroom, or at home.

SUMMARY

To create and conduct a lesson, teachers need to be mindful of a variety of components: appropriate and varied resources, a realistic idea of the time it takes to conduct the lesson, strategies to teach the lesson and differentiate it, what they will do and say during the lesson, and grouping configurations. This chapter, along with the repertoire of other tools in this book, provides teachers with a multitude of information and ideas to create and deliver meaningful, differentiated lessons.

6

Closing

Differentiated classrooms feel right to students who learn in different ways and at different rates and who bring to school different talents and interests. More significantly, such classrooms work better for a full range of students than do one-size-fits-all settings. Teachers in differentiated classrooms are more in touch with their students and approach teaching more as an art than as a mechanical exercise.

—Carol Tomlinson (1999)

Differentiation is a proactive, choreographed way to best meet the needs of all students in a classroom by challenging them appropriately at their varied ability levels and being cognizant enough of students' varied interests and learning styles to address them. It involves modifying and adjusting content, process, and product as we take into account what students are interested in, the way in which they learn best, and what they come to a classroom already knowing. It involves teachers approaching curriculum with a strong sense of what is most essential in what they are about to teach. Teachers need a keen handle on the standards and must craft guiding questions that elucidate them from a conceptual standpoint. These questions need to be at the forefront in their teaching so students realize the overall point to any lesson or unit at large.

Teachers, like students, are a differentiated group by virtue of their personalities, expertise, clientele, and teaching situations. Once you embrace the philosophy of differentiation and sound lesson design, I encourage you to begin at a comfortable pace so as not to be overwhelmed. And it is important for you to know that differentiation does not mean that every single lesson within a unit includes a differentiated content, process, and product for each and every student's area of interest, readiness level, and learning profile. In fact, differentiating to this extent may not even be necessary or prudent given the focus of a particular lesson or unit. Start at a place that makes sense to you and keep firmly abreast of the core curricular goals. As a suggestion, you might review each chapter of this book and hone your expertise in one particular area and start there. Change can happen gradually; grow at an acceptable pace for you. But make sure you set concrete, realistic goals, and commit to adhering to them.

My book is intended to assuage teachers who are fearful of differentiation, to empower teachers who want to differentiate better, to instill a sense of confidence in differentiating lessons, and also to deliver effective curriculum. In this book, I have taken you by the hand to help build or revise differentiated lessons and explain what good teaching looks like. I have chunked each component of a differentiated lesson design and provided examples across the content areas. You can apply and adapt what you have read to your own classroom situation by grade and subject area.

You are encouraged to review the References and Further Reading section, obtain books, and attend conferences and workshops to further your knowledge base in differentiation. The more well read and educated you are and the more you collaborate with colleagues and even students, the more willing and eager you will be to experiment with differentiation to continually expand your expertise. A natural by-product is that students will be more eager to learn, and their parents will be more thankful. Hence, you will feel an elevated sense of self-esteem for taking the initiative and implementing professional development derived from this book and other opportunities you have sought. May your journey be one full of wonderment, learning, action, and reflection.

References and Further Reading

Aronson, E. (1978). *The jigsaw classroom.* Beverly Hills, CA: Sage.

Barnard, S. (2005). *Transformational teaching: The key to authentic school improvement.* Omaha, NE: iUniverse.

Benson, J., et al. (1993). *Gateways to algebra and geometry: An integrated approach.* Evanston, IL: McDougal Littell.

Birch, D. (1988). *The king's chessboard.* New York: Puffin Books.

California Department of Education. (1994). *Differentiating the core curriculum and instruction to provide advanced learning opportunities.* Sacramento, CA: Author.

Campbell, B., & Campbell, L. (1999). *Multiple intelligences and student achievement: Success stories from six schools* (p. 69). Thousand Oaks, CA: Corwin Press.

Chapman, C., & King, R. (2003). *Differentiated instructional strategies for reading in the content areas.* Thousand Oaks, CA: Corwin Press.

Clarke, J. (1994). Pieces of the puzzle: The jigsaw method. In S. Sharan (Ed.), *Handbook of cooperative learning methods* (pp. 34–50). Westport, CT: Greenwood Press.

Clarke, J., Widerman, R., & Eadie, S. (1990). *Together we learn.* Scarborough, ON: Prentice Hall.

Cohen, B., & Lovejoy, B. (1982). *Seven daughters and seven sons.* New York: Macmillan.

Cohen, E. (1994). *Designing groupwork: Strategies for the heterogeneous classroom* (2nd ed.). New York: Teachers College Press.

Covey, S. (1989). *Seven habits of highly effective people.* New York: Free Press.

Daniels, H. (1994). *Literature circles: Voice and choice in the student-centered classroom.* Portland, ME: Stenhouse Publishers.

Drapeau, P. (2004). *Differentiated instruction: Making it work.* New York: Scholastic Teaching Resources.

Dunn, R., & Dunn, K. (1987). Dispelling outmoded beliefs about student learning. *Educational Leadership, 44*(6), 55–61.

Erickson, L. H. (2002). *Concept-based curriculum and instruction: Teaching beyond the facts.* Thousand Oaks, CA: Corwin Press.

Fisher, D., & Frey, N. (2007). *Checking for understanding: Formative assessment techniques for your classroom.* Alexandria, VA: Association for Supervision and Curriculum Development.

Forbes, E. (1943). *Johnny Tremain.* New York: Bantam Doubleday.

Forsten, C., Grant, J., & Hollas, B. (2003). *Differentiating textbooks: Strategies to improve student comprehension and motivation.* Peterborough, NH: Crystal Springs Books.

Gardner, H. (1993). *Multiple intelligences: The theory in practice.* New York: Basic Books.

Glass, K. (2005). *Curriculum design for writing instruction: Creating standards-based lessons and rubrics.* Thousand Oaks, CA: Corwin Press.

Glass, K. (2007). *Curriculum mapping: A step-by-step guide to creating curriculum year overviews.* Thousand Oaks, CA: Corwin Press.

Gregory, G. (2003). *Differentiated instructional strategies in practice: Training, implementation, and supervision.* Thousand Oaks, CA: Corwin Press.

Gregory, G. H., & Chapman, C. (2007). *Differentiated instructional strategies: One size doesn't fit all* (2nd ed.). Thousand Oaks, CA: Corwin Press.

Inspiration Software, Inc., Inspiration 8: www.inspiration.com

Jacobs, H. H. (1997). *Mapping the big picture: Integrating curriculum and assessment K–12.* Alexandria, VA: Association for Supervision and Curriculum Development.

Joyce, M., & Tallman, J. (1997). *Making the writing and research connection with the I-search process.* New York: Neal-Schuman Publishers.

Kagan, S. (1992, 1994). *Cooperative learning.* San Clemente, CA: Kagan Publishing.

Karwoski, G. L. (2006). *Quake!: Disaster in San Francisco, 1906.* Atlanta, GA: Peachtree Publishers.

Keeley, P. (2008). *Science formative assessment.* Thousand Oaks, CA: Corwin Press.

Kelly, R. (2000). Working with WebQuests: Making the Web accessible to students with disabilities. *Teaching Exceptional Children, 32*(6), 4–13.

Kierman, L. (producer). (1997). *Differentiating instruction: A video staff development set.* Alexandria, VA: Association for Supervision and Curriculum Development.

Knowles, M. (1986). *Using learning contracts.* San Francisco: Jossey-Bass.

Kurzweil 3000: www.kurzweiledu.com

Lyman, F. T. (1981). The responsive classroom discussion: The inclusion of all students. In A. Anderson (Ed.), *Mainstreaming digest* (pp. 109–113). College Park: University of Maryland Press.

Lyman, F. (1992). Think-pair-share, thinktrix, and weird facts. In N. Davidson & T. Worsham (Eds.), *Enhancing thinking through cooperative learning.* New York: Teachers College Press.

Macrorie, K. (1988). *The I-search paper.* Portsmouth, NH: Boynton/Cook Publishers.

Marzano, R., & Kendall, J. (2000). *Content knowledge: A compendium of standards and benchmarks for K–12 education* (3rd ed.). Aurora, CO: McREL.

McTighe, J., & O'Connor, K. (2005, November). Seven practices for effective learning. *Educational Leadership, 63*(3).

Myers, W. D. (2002). The treasure of Lemon Brown. In *Prentice Hall literature: Timeless voices, timeless themes* (pp. 475–484). Upper Saddle River, NJ: Pearson Education.

Palincsar, A. S. (1986). Reciprocal teaching. In *Teaching reading as thinking.* Oak Brook, IL: North Central Regional Educational Laboratory.

Palincsar, A. S., & Brown, A. L. (1985). Reciprocal teaching: Activities to promote read(ing) with your mind. In T. L. Harris & E. J. Cooper (Eds.), *Reading, thinking and concept development: Strategies for the classroom.* New York: The College Board.

Reading for the Blind & Dyslexic Web site: http://www.rfbd.org/www.librivox.org

Reis, S. M., Burns, D. E., & Renzulli, J. S. (1992). *Curriculum compacting: The complete guide to modifying the regular classroom for high-ability students.* Mansfield Center, CT: Creative Learning Press.

Santa, C. M. (1988). *Content reading including study systems.* Dubuque, IA: Kendall/Hunt.

Sharon, Y., & Sharon, S. (1992). *Expanding cooperative learning through group investigation.* New York: Teachers College Press.

Silver, H., Strong, R., & Perini, M. (2000). *So each may learn: Integrating learning styles and multiple intelligences.* Alexandria: VA: Association for Supervision and Curriculum Development.

Slavin, R. E. (1994). *Cooperative learning: Theory, research, and practice.* Boston: Allyn & Bacon.

Spandel, V. (2001). *Creating writers through 6-trait writing assessment and instruction* (3rd ed.). Reading, MA: Addison-Wesley-Longman.

Sternberg, R. (1996). *Successful intelligence: How practical and creative intelligence determines success in life.* New York: Simon & Schuster.

Taylor, M. D. (1997). *Roll of thunder, hear my cry.* New York: Puffin Books.

Thieman, G. Y. (2007, October 24). Genocide claiming a larger place in middle and high school lessons. *Education Week*.

Tomlinson, C. (1995). *How to differentiate instruction in mixed ability classrooms*. Alexandria, VA: Association for Supervision and Curriculum Development.

Tomlinson, C. (1996a). *Differentiating instruction for mixed-ability classrooms*. [An ASCD professional inquiry kit]. Alexandria, VA: Association for Supervision and Curriculum Development.

Tomlinson, C. (1996b). Good teaching for one and all: Does gifted education have an instructional identity? *Journal for the Education of the Gifted, 20*, 155–174.

Tomlinson, C. (1999). *The differentiated classroom: Responding to the needs of all learners*. Alexandria, VA: Association for Supervision and Curriculum Development.

Tomlinson, C. (2001). *How to differentiate instruction in mixed-ability classrooms* (2nd ed.). Alexandria, VA: Association for Supervision and Curriculum Development.

Tomlinson, C. (2003). *Fulfilling the promise of the differentiated classroom: Strategies and tools for responsive teaching*. Alexandria, VA: Association for Supervision and Curriculum Development.

Tomlinson, C., & Eidson, C. (2003). *Differentiation in practice: A resource guide for differentiating curriculum*. Alexandria, VA: Association for Supervision and Curriculum Development.

Tomlinson, C., et al. (2002). *The parallel curriculum: A design to develop high potential and challenge high-ability learners*. Thousand Oaks, CA: Corwin Press, with the National Association for Gifted Children.

Tomlinson, C., & McTighe, J. (2006). *Integrating differentiated instruction + understanding by design*. Alexandria, VA: Association for Supervision and Curriculum Development.

Wiggins, G., & McTighe, J. (1998). *Understanding by design*. Alexandria, VA: Association for Supervision and Curriculum Development.

Wiggins, G., & McTighe, J. (2005). *Understanding by design* (2nd ed.). Alexandria, VA: Association for Supervision and Curriculum Development.

Winebrenner, S. (2001). *Teaching gifted kids in the regular classroom: Strategies and techniques every teacher can use to meet the academic needs of the gifted and talented*. Minneapolis, MN: Free Spirit Publishing.

CONTENT STANDARDS

Education World (access to all state standards), http://www.education-world .com/standards/state/index.shtml

Mid-continent Research for Education and Learning (McREL), Phone: (303) 337-0990, http://www.mcrel.org/standards-benchmarks/

National Center on Educational Outcomes (access to all state standards), http:// education.umn.edu/nceo/TopicAreas/Standards/StatesStandards.htm

The National Council of Teachers of English (NCTE), Phone: (217) 328-3870 or (877) 369-6283, http://www.ncte.org/about/over/standards/110846.htm (joint effort with NCTE and International Reading Association [IRA]).

Science Content Standards for California Public Schools Kindergarten Through Grade Twelve. California Department of Education, 2000. http://www.cde.ca.gov/ be/st/ss/documents/sciencestnd.pdf

GRAPHIC ORGANIZER WEB SITES

http://www.eduplace.com/graphicorganizer/

http://www.edhelper.com/teachers/graphic_organizers.htm

http://www.nvo.com/ecnewletter/graphicorganizers/

http://www.region15.org/curriculum/graphicorg.html

Index

CORWIN

A SAGE Company

The Corwin logo—a raven striding across an open book—represents the union of courage and learning. Corwin is committed to improving education for all learners by publishing books and other professional development resources for those serving the field of PreK–12 education. By providing practical, hands-on materials, Corwin continues to carry out the promise of its motto: **"Helping Educators Do Their Work Better."**